THE GREAT AMERICAN TOFU COOKBOOK

HOW TO USE HIGH-PROTEIN, LOW-CALORIE, CHOLESTEROL-FREE TOFU TO MAKE AMERICA'S FAVORITE ETHNIC DISHES, INCLUDING: LASAGNE, STROGANOFF, CREOLE, GOULASH, ENCHILADAS, BLINTZES, GUACAMOLE, CHEESECAKE, RICE PUDDING, AND OVER 100 MORE.

PATRICIA GADDIS McGRUTER

AUTUMN PRESS

Published by Autumn Press, Inc.,
with editorial offices at
1318 Beacon Street
Brookline, Massachusetts 02146

Library of Congress Catalog Number: 79-51817
ISBN: 0-914398-40-7
Printed in the United States of America
Typeset at dnh, Cambridge, Massachusetts

Illustrated by Stephanie Fleischer
Book design and typography by Beverly Stiskin

THE GREAT AMERICAN
TOFU COOKBOOK

Table of Contents

Acknowledgments

With special thanks to
   Mom and Dad, for loving, feeding and teaching me;
   Delpine Perry, for her wonderful gourmet cooking;
   Charles Perry, for all the warmth he had to give;
   Debbie Balmuth, for staying in touch;
   Rosielie, for her many special desserts and
      fine company on those sleepless nights;
   Dean, for his wit, wisdom and support;
   Aleia, for her good timing;
      and especially
   Douglas, for his never-ending encouragement,
      ideas and Love;
   and for Bucky, because of who she is.

Introduction

I first heard of tofu ten years ago, when a favorite friend informed me that it was an excellent non-animal source of protein, a point we were very enthusiastic about because of our vegetarian diet. But his knowledge of this "new" food product ended there. It's an excellent source of protein, but what is it and where do I go to buy it? When I asked for it at the local markets the surprised looks on the clerks' faces told me they were even more unfamiliar with it than I was, and not being one who persists in feeling ridiculous, I quit asking.

A few months later, when tofu had become a haze in my memory, a leisurely trip to a new market found me holding an unfamiliar carton stamped with the words "TOFU" and "Soybean Curd." Inside the carton was what looked like a block of white cheese completely submerged in water. My uninitiated tastebuds told me to leave it there, but my curiosity and protein-hungry diet convinced me to try it at least once.

When I got home, I put my tofu in the back of the refrigerator, semi-hoping it would magically prepare itself into something "edible." I had no idea what to do with it, and no recipes to help me along.

Our first meal was scrambled tofu, based on the concept of scrambled eggs (what else do you do with something when you're not sure of what you're doing?). I tossed the tofu into a frying pan, seasoned it cautiously, then liberally, with almost everything I had on hand, and dressed it up with fresh mushrooms, green chilies, and sliced green onions. To our surprise, we loved it and from that point on, cooking with tofu became an adventure for me.

For the next few months we ate tofu in every "scrambled" way I could think of, and it was during this experimental period that I discovered tofu's unique adaptability to so many different flavors. I had been a vegetarian for several years and had been continually frustrated by the lack of "taste" variety in the bean and grain dishes I served. I have to admit that I really enjoyed the flavor of meat and had an extensive collection of gourmet

9

recipes which, because I was unable to convert them to a meatless diet, were hidden away in a never-opened drawer. Tofu became the key to reviving them. On its own tofu is very bland, with a creamy neutral flavor so pure as to be almost tasteless; and therein lies the secret. Because of its neutrality it readily absorbs the essence of what it's being cooked or seasoned with. Tofu puts the cook in total control over the outcome of a dish because it can be "transformed" into virtually anything!

The more I cooked with tofu, the more ambitious I became. I discovered that if I mashed it up a bit and added a little mayonnaise and seasonings I could make great Tofu Salad Sandwiches at half the cost of Egg Salad—and with virtually no cholesterol! If I whipped it and varied the seasonings, it replaced ricotta and Jack cheeses in the lasagna, manicotti and enchiladas that I loved to bake—at half the calories. Diced and lightly sautéed, tofu became the "meaty" protein addition to many of my favorite casseroles; reshaped, braised and dressed with tomatoes, peppers and onions it became my cherished Hungarian Goulash.

The publication in 1975 of *The Book of Tofu*, by Bill Shurtleff and Akiko Aoyagi, opened wide the world of tofu for me as it did for many thousands of others. A veritable encyclopedia, the book holds a revered station in my kitchen and on my reference shelf. Through it I learned of all the shapes and forms that tofu takes—its ability to be pressed or molded, sauced or stuffed, deep-fried or baked—and how to make tofu at home. At the same time, the book stimulated the increasingly wide distribution of tofu in natural food stores, oriental markets, and even many standard supermarkets across the country, so that today tofu is relatively easy to come by.

For those of you who know tofu already, it is hoped that this book will show you some pathways you haven't traveled. For those of you who are still saying "what is it?" here's hoping that this book will make your first introduction to tofu less ominous than was mine. And for those of you who could not care less whether tofu is a healthful alternative for meat or a food that is truly good for you, this book could convince you to try tofu anyway, just because it tastes so good.

Tofu has been a staple of the East Asian diet for several thousand years. Its sudden rise in popularity in the west is due, in large part, to the great upsurge of interest in diet coupled with the steady rise in the cost of meat. The average American is a meat-eater and has little idea of how to prepare a good-tasting meal without the use of animal products. In fact, many people believe that a meal without meat, eggs or cheese just couldn't taste good, let alone be nutritious. Even many gourmet vegetarian cooks rely heavily on the use of cheese and eggs in their main dishes, which is fine for some people but not for those who are trying to watch their weight, cut down on their cholesterol intake, or save money. High in protein, low in calories and cholesterol, and the ultimate in great taste when prepared creatively, tofu is the perfect food for meat-lover, health-enthusiast, penny-pincher, and vegetarian alike.

For the weight conscious, 8 ounces of tofu contains only 147 calories; an equal weight of eggs has about three times as many calories while the same amount of beef has almost four and a half times as many. Next to mung and soy sprouts, tofu has the lowest ratio of calories to protein found in any known plant food. I've found that 4 ounces of tofu is a hearty serving for almost anyone, so it averages out at approximately 75 calories per serving.

For the vegetarians who are looking for more protein in their diets, 8 ounces of tofu provides 27 percent of the daily adult protein requirement and only 5 grams of carbohydrates. Combined with grains, whole wheat breads, noodles, or corn tortillas, a complete, easily digested protein is available. In addition, it provides 38 percent of the average adult daily calcium requirement, a real concern for those who have eliminated dairy products from their diet.*

Some people have to worry about their cholesterol intake and those of us who don't, perhaps should. Tofu is low in saturated fats and entirely free of cholesterol. It is high in both linoleic acid, an essential fatty acid not synthesized by the body, and natural lecithin. Lecithin performs the functions of metabolizing, dispersing and eliminating deposits of cholesterol accumulated in the body. Tofu is also a very easily digested protein, making it the perfect food for the elderly, for babies, and for people convalescing from surgery or illness.

No matter how wonderful a food is for the well-being of our bodies, if it doesn't taste good we generally won't eat it. Fortunately, tofu is one of those healthful foods that tastes good too. Taste-wise, tofu is not a meat substitute. It does not, in itself, resemble meat, fish, or poultry in any way. But it can replace these meats, and cheese, in virtually any recipe from soups and salads to main dishes and desserts, so you don't have to forego your treasured family recipes to learn an entire new way of cooking. With the price of meat skyrocketing and its quality dropping, even the staunchest omnivore would benefit by giving tofu a second glance. Today, in most parts of the United States, the price of tofu per pound, enough for a satisfying meal for three, ranges between 55 and 75 cents. Try buying a pound of hamburger for that price!

Tofu appeals to a wide variety of people because it is so very versatile. I love to cook foods with a foreign flavor. They lend an aura of romance,

---

* William Shurtleff and Akiko Aoyagi, *The Book of Tofu* (Autumn Press: 1975), p. 38.

legend and mystique to a meal. Because tofu is so bland, it can adapt to an international array of dishes from spicy Tofu Ratatouille, Stroganoff, and Tofu and Mushroom Crêpes to sweet and creamy Tofu Blintzes, Chocolate Mousse Cheesecake, and Rice Pudding. The magical quality of tofu is that it gives the cook the ultimate freedom to be creative—the only limiting factors are one's daring and/or the contents of the spice cupboard. In fact, the biggest secret in versatility with tofu cooking is one's ability to be creative with herbs, spices, and sauces. Blending herbs and spices requires some skill, a discerning palate, and a lot of practice. In cooking with tofu, you are free to be as daring—or cautious—as you please. Each person likes food to varying degrees of "spiciness." My tastes may not be your tastes, so use the recipes presented here as the basic guide and adjust the seasonings to your own liking.

When working with herbs and spices it is very important to buy the best available. Buy pure (unchemicalized) seasonings; if you're lucky enough to have fresh herbs available, so much the better. Buying herbs and spices in bulk is much cheaper than buying small quantities prepackaged. To retain their freshness, store your seasonings in darkly tinted jars and bottles away from heat and light. The volatile oils in herbs and spices are easily destroyed and must be pampered if they are to perform the task expected of them in cooking. Check your seasonings regularly. If their color has faded and your nose has to search endlessly for an aroma, they need to be replaced.

Be as careful shopping for other ingredients as you are at buying herbs and spices. Almost all the ingredients used in these recipes can be bought in your local supermarket, but please be sure to buy them in their *purest* form. Our bodies thrive on good, wholesome, living foods and were not designed to handle an excess of anything—including sugar and chemical additives. Love yourself and your family, and pay attention to what you're buying. Become a label reader. Items like canned tomatoes, tomato sauce, chilies, mayonnaise, mustard, ketchup, jams, jellies and frozen fruits can all be bought free of sugar or chemical preservatives, often in regular supermarkets. Items like cold-pressed oils, shoyu (natural soy sauce), miso (soybean paste), tahini, carob, agar and whole wheat, soy or spinach noodles most often need to be bought in natural food stores or food co-ops. A good reference book for supermarket shopping is *The Supermarket Handbook: Access to Whole Foods* by Nikki and David Goldbeck (Signet Press).

Preparatory Techniques

Today you can find many varieties of tofu, including fresh, grilled, fermented, and deep-fried, just to name a few. In my recipes, I have used only two of these, fresh and deep-fried tofu.

There are several different kinds of fresh tofu, and the main differences are in their firmness. Soft tofu, or *kinugoshi*, is velvety-smooth and is good for use in puddings, cream soups, and dishes in which the tofu needs little handling. Medium-firm tofu (what I refer to as "regular tofu" in the recipes, and is often called Dow Foo, or Japanese-style tofu) is tofu that has been drained of its excess liquid and compressed to form a block. Hard, or firm, tofu (also referred to as Chinese-style tofu) is drained and compressed even more than regular tofu, and is the easiest form to work with because it holds its shape well during handling and cooking.

I use regular (medium-firm) and hard tofu in these recipes, but they are basically interchangeable. Just remember that if you use regular tofu where firm tofu is called for, you should increase the pressing time by 15 to 30 minutes in order to attain the right consistency.

All fresh tofu comes submerged in water. If it is bought in a local supermarket or natural food store, it usually comes packaged in plastic tubs, many with nutritional information and types of solidifier listed. If the tofu is purchased in a tofu shop, the shopkeeper usually packs it for you on the spot in small cardboard containers. At many Oriental markets and food co-ops you should bring your own jars. Be sure to refrigerate the tofu and keep it covered with water for freshness. Prepackaged tofu will usually keep in the refrigerator for a week to ten days, but once it has been opened, or if you bring your tofu home in containers or jars, you must change the water every day, and use the tofu within several days to enjoy maximum freshness.

The flavor and texture of tofu is determined, in part, by the type of solidifier used. There are several, the most common being calcium sulfate, a chemical, and nigari (bittern), made from salt water that has had most of the salt removed. Tofu solidified with nigari is preferable, so check the label or ask your grocer to be sure. Also, the fresher the tofu, the sweeter its flavor. Warm homemade tofu has a sweet and creamy flavor that quickly begins to fade once the tofu is refrigerated. If you can't make the homemade variety, check the date stamped on the package to insure that you are getting the freshest tofu possible.

The recipes in this book also call for deep-fried tofu, including agé, deep-fried tofu, and ganmo. Deep-fried tofu and ganmo are easily made at home but agé, highly compressed tofu fried in hot oil until puffy and hollow, requires a little more skill in preparing properly. If you are lucky enough to have a tofu shop in your town, I suggest you purchase your agé there for maximum ease and convenience. Well wrapped, agé will keep for several weeks in the refrigerator and up to a month in the freezer. Tofu's taste and texture are also affected by the manner in which it is prepared before its actual use in cooking. It can be squeezed, drained, pressed, parboiled, scrambled, crumbled, reshaped or frozen.

Like anything new and different, tofu takes some time to get to know. Keep in mind that working with any new medium requires practice. Cooking with tofu is easy but, like all good cooking, it requires care. If you exert the effort, the rewards are guaranteed.

Basic Tofu Recipe

Makes 1¼ pounds

1½ cups dry soybeans washed, soaked in 6 cups water for 10 hours, rinsed and drained

16 cups water, approximately

1¾ to 2½ teaspoons granulated nigari or Epsom salts; or ½ cup lemon juice or vinegar

Place a colander inside a large pot and line it with a moistened coarse-weave dishcloth or sack. Line a 2-quart strainer or perforated box with a moistened fine-weave cotton cloth.

Heat 7½ cups of water in a large pot over medium-high heat. Combine ½ of the soaked soybeans with 2 cups of water in a blender and purée for 3 minutes; add the puree to the heating water. Purée and add the remaining beans in the same way, stirring constantly. Bring the contents of the pot just to a boil (it will foam quickly); pour into the lined colander or sack. Gather the corners of the cloth, twist closed, and press firmly with the base of a jar to extract the soymilk (it is very hot). Combine the pulp in the sack (okara) with 3 cups of water; pour back into the sack, re-press, and set pulp aside for use in other recipes.

Pour all the extracted soymilk into the cooking pot and, stirring constantly, bring to a boil; reduce heat and simmer for 5 minutes. Remove pan from heat; dissolve the nigari or other solidifier in 1 cup of water and slowly stir into the hot soymilk. Cover and allow to stand for 3 minutes, or until the milk has separated into soft white curds and pale-yellow whey. Gently press a small fine-mesh strainer into the pot and allow several cups of whey to collect in it. Ladle out all of the whey and save it for use in soup stocks or to clean pots and pans when finished (it makes dishes sparkle!). Ladle the curds into the cloth-lined 2-quart strainer or perforated box; press under a lid with a 1-pound weight for 15 minutes. Place the finished tofu in a container of cold water for 3 minutes; cut into portions and chill.

Store tofu in a container of cold water, with a lid, until ready to use. It will stay fresh in the refrigerator for 5 days if the water is changed daily. A firmer tofu, used for deep-fried, frozen or grilled tofu can be prepared by simply increasing the pressing weight to 4 pounds for 15 minutes.

Tofu has a high water content which sometimes seems bothersome, but actually makes for tofu's incredible versatility: it can be parboiled, pressed or drained for a firm texture; squeezed for a creamy-light texture; or scrambled, crumbled, reshaped, or frozen for a "meaty" texture.

Parboiling; Salted Water Method

Boil 2 cups of water; add ½ teaspoon salt, drop in a 12-ounce cake of tofu, and return to a boil. Remove the pan from the heat and allow to stand for 2 to 3 minutes. Remove the tofu, discarding the water. (The addition of salt to the water seasons the tofu slightly and makes it firmer.)

Parboiling is used to warm tofu before serving it topped with sauces; or to freshen older tofu; or to make firm tofu for use in cooking or salads.

Pressing

Slice the tofu cake in half or into fourths, depending on the recipe; place the slices on newspaper lined with paper towel. Place a small cutting board and a 2- to 4-pound weight on the tofu and allow to stand for 20 to 60 minutes.

Pressing is used for tofu that will be sliced or deep-fried.

Draining

Place the tofu cake in a colander inside a 1- or 2-quart flat bottomed container. Cover and refrigerate for 1 hour. Pat dry with a towel.

Draining makes the tofu firmer and helps to preserve flavor. Do not drain for more than 12 hours. Keep refrigerated.

Squeezing

Place drained, parboiled or pressed tofu in the center of a large dish towel or tofu draining sack; gather the corners to form a sack. Twist the sack closed and squeeze the tofu firmly, kneading for 2 to 3 minutes to expel as much moisture as possible without squeezing out the tofu. Empty into a bowl.

Squeezing is used to make mashed tofu, resembling cottage cheese in texture.

Scrambling

Place the tofu in a skillet and break into small pieces with a wooden spatula. Cook over medium heat for 5 minutes, stirring and breaking the tofu into smaller and smaller pieces. Stir continuously until the curds and whey separate. Pour the tofu into a strainer and allow the curds to drain for 3 to 4 minutes.

Scrambling causes a further separation of curds and whey resulting in a texture similar to that of squeezed tofu, but firmer and crumblier.

Crumbling

Combine one 12-ounce cake of tofu and 1 cup of water in a saucepan. Place over medium heat and bring to a boil, stirring constantly to break the tofu into very small pieces. Reduce heat and simmer for 1 to 2 minutes. Pour the contents of the pan into a colander lined with a large dishtowel and placed in the sink. Gather the corners of the towel to form a sack; twist closed. Press the rapped tofu against the colander with a jar or potato masher to expel as much water as possible. Place the tofu in a bowl and allow to cool for 3 to 4 minutes; break into very small pieces with the fingertips.

Crumbled tofu has the same texture as lightly sautéed hamburger—firm, light, and fluffy. It is ideal for use in salads, egg and grain dishes, sauces, and casseroles.

Reshaping

Combine two 12-ounce cakes of tofu and 1 teaspoon sea salt in a sauce-pan, mixing well. Cook over medium heat, stirring constantly, for 4 minutes, or until the tofu begins to boil. Pour the tofu into a colander lined with a large dishtowel and placed in the sink; drain for 3 to 4 minutes. Transfer the cloth to a cutting board and carefully fold the edges over the tofu. Shape the tofu into a cake 5 inches square and 1 inch thick. Place in a cool place with a pan filled with 3 to 4 quarts of water on top of it; press for 1 to 2 hours. Unwrap the tofu and cut or rewrap in a dry towel. Refrig-erate until ready to use.

Reshaping gives the tofu a firm cohesive consistency like natural cheese or ham. Use it in recipes calling for french-fry-sized pieces, which hold their shape during cooking or tossing.

Freezing

If store-bought in plastic tubs, tofu may be frozen in its original container. Once frozen, its texture changes from custard-like to spongy and can be used like hamburger. Thaw completely before using; drain, rinse and squeeze dry.

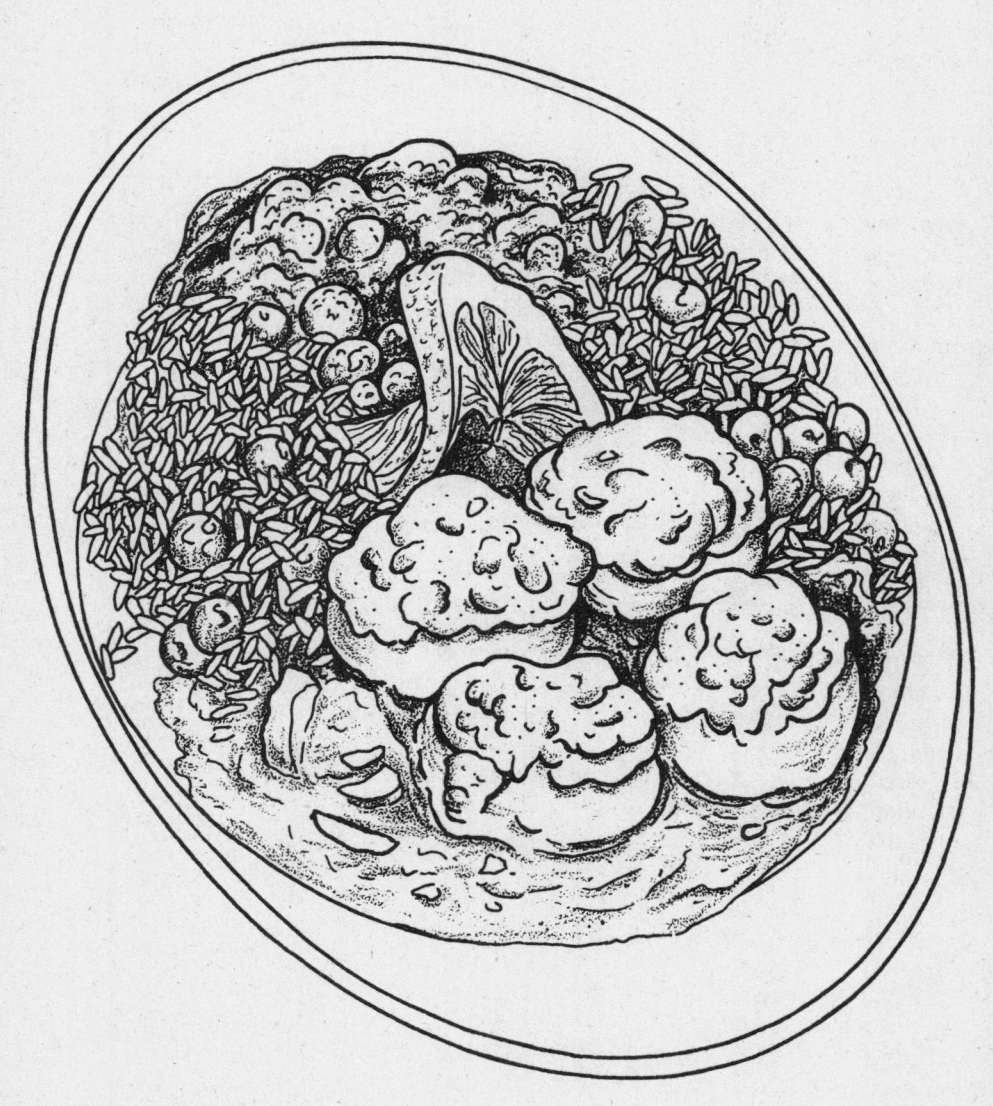

Appetizers

Tofu-Stuffed Mushroom Caps

Serves 3 to 4

1 cup regular tofu, squeezed
¼ cup fresh parsley, finely chopped
½ teaspoon sea salt
Freshly ground black pepper
¼ teaspoon tarragon
¼ teaspoon chervil (optional)
3 dashes nutmeg
2 tablespoons sour cream
1 tablespoon fresh lemon juice, strained
4 tablespoons olive oil
18 medium-sized mushrooms
½ cup mozzarella cheese, cut into ¼-inch
   pieces

Preheat oven to 400°F. Place the tofu in a large mixing bowl; with a wooden spoon, beat in the parsley, spices, sour cream and lemon juice until the mixture is very smooth. Remove the stems from the mushrooms and mince enough for 4 tablespoonfuls; add to the tofu mixture and stir. Set the tofu aside.

In a large skillet, heat the oil over medium heat until lightly hazy. Add the mushroom caps and fry for 2 minutes; turn the caps over and fry for 1 to 2 minutes more, or until lightly browned. Remove the caps with a slotted spoon and drain for 5 to 6 seconds on newspaper or paper towels. Fill each mushroom cap with the tofu mixture and top with a piece of mozzarella cheese. Arrange the caps side by side in a shallow baking dish. Bake for 8 minutes, or until the filling bubbles. Remove from the oven and place caps under the broiler for 5 seconds to brown the cheese topping. Serve at once.

Kalindi's Kraze

Serves 3 to 4

6 ounces regular tofu, drained for 30 minutes
1 heaping tablespoon Kome Miso (brown rice
    miso)
2 whole green onions, finely chopped
2 tablespoons unflavored yoghurt
2 heaping tablespoons "good-tasting" brewer's
    yeast flakes
1 clove garlic, minced
1 carrot, grated
1 handful sunflower seeds, raw or roasted
1 teaspoon shoyu (natural soy sauce)
Dash of paprika and cayenne (red) pepper
Sea salt to taste

In a medium bowl, mash the tofu into small pieces. Add the remaining ingredients and mix well. If too thick, add more yoghurt. Serve spread on whole wheat bread, topped with sprouts and tomatoes, or as a dip with wedges of pita bread.

VARIATION: Thin with a little water, blend, and use as salad dressing.

Guacamole Dip

        Makes 3 to 4 cups
    8 ounces regular tofu
    4 ripe avocados
    2 small tomatoes, diced
    1 onion, diced
    2 cloves garlic, minced
    4 yellow chilies, chopped with seeds included
        (leave out the seeds for a milder dip)
    1 tablespoon fresh lemon juice
    Sea salt to taste

Whirl the tofu in a blender at medium speed for 2 minutes until smooth, stopping when necessary to scrape down the sides with a spatula. In a mixing bowl, mash the avocados until almost smooth; add the tofu. Stir in the remaining ingredients. Chill. Do not make the dip too far in advance as the avocados turn brown if allowed to stand, although the taste will not be impaired.

VARIATION: To serve the Guacamole as a salad, shred ½ head of lettuce into the dip and mix. This makes an excellent filling for tacos, garnished with jalapeño chilies and black olives.

Rice-Filled Agé

Makes 36 appetizers or 9 servings

⅓ cup white wine vinegar

1 tablespoon honey or to taste

2 cups cooked brown rice, hot

½ cup grated carrot

¼ cup whole green onions, chopped

1 handful raw or toasted sunflower seeds

9 agé

Combine the vinegar and honey. Place the rice in a large bowl. Stir in the vinegar mixture and allow to cool. Add the carrot, onions and sunflower seeds, mixing well.

Rinse the agé in hot water and drain. Cut off one end of each age, pull out the soft interior and stuff with the rice mixture. Cover and chill. Serve whole agé as a meal or slice into pieces to serve as appetizers.

Tofu Hummus

Makes 2½ to 3 cups

½ pound regular tofu, drained for 20 minutes

1 cup cooked garbanzo beans (chick peas),
   drained

1 cup tahini

½ to ¾ cup lemon juice, freshly squeezed and
   strained

1 to 2 teaspoons sea salt

2 cloves garlic, minced

Fresh parsley, chopped, to garnish

Combine all the ingredients except the parsley in a blender; blend at medium speed for 2 to 3 minutes until smooth, stopping when necessary to scrape down the sides with a spatula. Refrigerate the mixture for 3 to 4 hours.

Adjust the seasoning and garnish with parsley. Serve as a dip with raw vegetables and wedges of pita bread or as a spread on crackers.

Deep-Fried Rice and Tofu Balls

Serves 6

2 eggs

2 cups cooked brown rice, flavored with basil,
  oregano and thyme while cooking, or 2
  cups leftover rice pilaf

8 ounces regular tofu, squeezed and kneaded
  for 5 minutes

1 clove garlic, minced

½ teaspoon sea salt

½ teaspoon summer savory

½ teaspoon crushed basil

¾ cup fine, dry, whole wheat bread crumbs

Cold-pressed soy oil for frying

In a large mixing bowl, beat the eggs lightly with a fork; add the rice or pilaf and stir thoroughly, taking care not to mash the rice. In a separate bowl, combine the tofu and the spices, kneading to blend.

Place 1 tablespoon of the tofu mixture over 1 tablespoon of the rice mixture and top with another tablespoon of rice mixture. Shape into a ball; roll in the bread crumbs and place on wax paper. Prepare all the balls and refrigerate for ½ hour.

In a wok or deep kettle, heat approximately 3 inches of oil to 375°F. Preheat the oven to 250°F.; line a baking dish with paper towels and place in the oven. Deep-fry the rice-tofu balls, 4 at a time, for 5 minutes or until golden brown. Transfer to the dish in the oven to keep warm until all the balls are fried. Serve immediately.

Tofu Strips with Spicy Peanut Sauce

Serves 4

1½ pounds regular tofu, reshaped

2 tablespoons + ½ teaspoon cold-pressed soy
oil

3 tablespoons natural smooth-style peanut
butter

¼ cup shoyu (natural soy sauce)

3 tablespoons date or raw sugar or 2 tablespoons honey

1 tablespoon cold-pressed sesame or soy oil

1 teaspoon garlic, minced

½ to ¾ teaspoon cayenne pepper

Cut the reshaped tofu into french-fry-sized pieces. With a pastry brush,
lightly brush all sides of the tofu pieces with approximately ½ teaspoon of
the soy oil. Place under a broiler and broil on both sides until crispy
golden brown. Place in a 225°F. oven to keep warm.

In a mixing bowl, mix the peanut butter and the remaining 2 tablespoons of soy oil until smooth. Add the remaining ingredients and stir
until velvety smooth. Cover and chill if prepared in advance, but warm to
room temperature before serving. Remove the tofu strips from the oven.
Serve with the dipping sauce on the side or poured over the strips.

Tofu in Coconut-Milk Sauce

In Brazil this dish is served as an appetizer or as part of a large dinner including several other main dishes, rice and vegetables. It traditionally uses shrimp.

Serves 4

Grated fresh meat from 1 coconut (about 2
   cups)
1½ cups boiling water
2 tablespoons butter
1½ pounds firm tofu, patted dry and cut into
   1½-inch cubes
3 tablespoons onion, chopped
Sea salt and pepper to taste
2 tablespoons rice flour
2 tablespoons cold water
1 tablespoon coconut milk (from the fresh
   coconut)

Combine the grated coconut and boiling water; allow to stand for 15 minutes. Strain the coconut, pressing out and reserving the juice. Melt the butter in a heavy skillet over medium-low heat; add the tofu and onions and sauté for 3 minutes, stirring constantly. Season to taste with salt and pepper; remove the tofu from the skillet. Add the reserved coconut juice to the onion-butter mixture and heat to boiling. In a small bowl, mix the rice flour and cold water and add to the hot coconut juice. Cook over medium heat for 4 minutes, stirring constantly until thickened. Reduce heat, cover, and simmer for 10 minutes. Stir in the coconut milk and sautéed tofu and heat through. Adjust seasoning to taste. Stir in ½ cup of the reserved coconut meat. Serve immediately.

Fried Tofu Balls

Crispy on the outside, creamy on the inside, these balls may be served as an appetizer or with steamed vegetables and brown rice for a light meal.

Serves 4 to 5

1 pound regular tofu, squeezed
1 large clove garlic, minced
1 teaspoon sea salt
⅛ teaspoon black pepper
½ teaspoon summer savory
½ teaspoon oregano
1 egg, slightly beaten
½ cup milk, dairy or soy
1 cup dry, crushed whole wheat bread crumbs
2 to 3 tablespoons cold-pressed olive oil
2½ tablespoons fresh lemon juice (strained)

In a bowl, knead the tofu for 5 minutes. Add the spices and knead for 3 to 4 minutes more. Roll the tofu into walnut-sized balls. Dip each ball into the lightly beaten egg, then into the milk, and roll in the bread crumbs. In a skillet, heat the oil. Add the tofu balls and fry for 4 to 5 seconds on each side until golden brown. Remove and drain on paper towels. Spear the tofu balls with toothpicks; sprinkle with lemon juice. Serve on a warmed platter.

Stuffed Sopaipillas
(*so-pah-pee-yahs*)

These Mexican treats make a delicious appetizer or main dish served with a hot platter of refried beans and rice.

Makes 4 dozen

Sopaipillas:

1 tablespoon dry yeast
¼ cup warm water (approximately 110°F.)
1½ cups soy or dairy milk
3 tablespoons butter or margarine (such as Willow Run soy margarine)
1½ teaspoons sea salt
2 tablespoons date or turbinado sugar
Approximately 4 cups unsifted unbleached white flour
1 cup whole wheat flour
Cold-pressed soy oil for deep frying

Stuffing:

2 to 3 tablespoons cold-pressed soy oil
2 onions, thinly sliced
4 cloves garlic, minced
4 pounds firm tofu, drained for ½ hour and patted dry
2 small cans Ortega chilies, diced
3 teaspoons cuminos
Shoyu (natural soy sauce) or sea salt and pepper to taste
3 teaspoons chili powder
½ cup cilantro or parsley, minced

Sopaipillas: In a large mixing bowl, dissolve the yeast in the warm water. Combine the milk, margarine, sea salt and sugar in a saucepan over low heat and heat until milk is lukewarm (approximately 110°F.). Add to the dissolved yeast. Beat in 3 cups of the unbleached flour and all of the whole wheat flour. With a wooden spoon, add more unbleached flour until the dough is sticky and stiff; turn onto a floured board and knead, adding flour as necessary, until dough is smooth and no longer sticky. Place the dough in a buttered bowl and turn to butter the top. Cover and allow to stand at room temperature for 1 hour.

Punch the dough down; cover and chill if not frying immediately. Knead the dough again on a lightly floured board to expel air; divide into 3 or 4 portions. Roll out each portion to about ⅛ inch thick; cut into 3-inch squares, place on lightly floured pans, and cover. The dough can stand at room temperature for up to 5 minutes; otherwise refrigerate.

In a wide, deep frying pan, kettle or wok, heat 2 inches of soy oil to 350°F. Fry the sopaipillas, 2 or 3 at a time, until the bread puffs; turn 3 or 4 times with a slotted spoon until pale golden on both sides. Remove and drain on a paper towel.

Stuffing: Pour the oil into a large heavy frying pan and heat over medium heat. Add the onions and garlic and sauté until tender. Add the tofu, crumbling it into the pan and breaking it into small pieces with a fork while cooking. Mix in the chilies, cuminos and shoyu or salt and pepper, stirring frequently with a wooden spatula. Cook for 15 minutes or until light and fluffy. Remove pan from heat; add the chili powder and stir well. Stir in the cilantro or parsley.

Cut each sopaipilla diagonally to form two triangles. Stuff each half with a rounded tablespoon of the stuffing. Serve immediately or keep in a warm oven until ready to serve. If prepared in advance, refrigerate or freeze. To reheat, bake uncovered in a 325°F. oven for 15 minutes, turning once, until heated through. Garnish with black olives and grated Jack cheese for a special treat.

Tofu Mustard Shish Kebabs

Tofu is a wonderful replacement in this dish that traditionally uses lamb.

Serves 4 to 6
3 tablespoons Dijon-style mustard (containing
    only natural ingredients)
2 tablespoons white wine vinegar
2 tablespoons cold-pressed olive oil
½ teaspoon rosemary
½ teaspoon sage
2 to 3 cloves garlic, minced
Sea salt and pepper to taste
2 pounds firm tofu, patted dry and cut into
    1-inch cubes

In a medium-sized bowl, combine the mustard, vinegar, oil, and spices, mixing well. Add the tofu cubes and sprinkle lightly with salt and pepper; marinate in the refrigerator for at least 3 hours or overnight, turning the tofu frequently.

Skewer the tofu cubes on wooden skewers that have been soaked in water to prevent burning. Cook under the broiler or over coals until brown and fragrant, basting often with the marinade. Serve immediately. Accompany with grilled vegetables such as green or red peppers, eggplant and mushrooms and a bulghur pilaf.

Anticuchos

Serves 6

Marinade:

1 cup red wine vinegar

2 cloves garlic, chopped

1 tablespoon cuminos

2 fresh red chilies, chopped

Sea salt and pepper to taste

1½ pounds firm tofu, drained, pressed and cut
   into 1½-inch squares

2 dried red chilies

1 tablespoon achiote seeds (available in Latin
   American markets)

½ cup cold-pressed olive oil

Combine all the marinade ingredients in a mixing bowl. Add the tofu cubes and allow to soak overnight.

Tear the chilies into small pieces and soak in boiling water to cover for ½ hour. Place the achiote seeds in a blender and grind at high speed to a fine powder. Add the chilies, their soaking liquid and the olive oil and blend at medium speed for 2 to 3 minutes, stopping when necessary to scrape down the sides with a spatula.

Skewer the tofu on small wooden skewers that have been soaked in water to prevent burning. Cook the tofu over coals or under a broiler until golden brown, basting often with the achiote mixture. Serve immediately with tortillas, sliced onions and chopped tomatoes.

Texas Broiled Tofu

This dish is traditionally made with shrip, found abundantly in Texas along the Gulf of Mexico.

Serves 4
1 cup cold-pressed olive oil
¼ cup fresh lemon juice, strained
2 to 3 large cloves garlic, crushed
1 pound firm tofu, drained, pressed and cut
    into 1-inch cubes
¼ cup fresh parsley, finely chopped
Sea salt and pepper to taste

In a medium-sized mixing bowl, combine the oil, lemon juice and garlic. Drop in the tofu cubes and marinate for at least 12 hours.

Skewer the tofu on small wooden skewers that have been soaked in water to prevent burning. Cook under a broiler or over coals for 3 to 5 minutes until the tofu is a delicate brown. Arrange the tofu on a platter and sprinkle with parsley, salt and pepper. Save the marinade to baste vegetables or add additional spices and use as a salad dressing. Serve with skewered vegetables such as tomatoes, eggplant, onions and green peppers, barbecued separately to taste.

Soups

Hearty Vegetable Soup

Serves 6 to 8
2 tablespoons olive oil
2 medium onions, chopped
1 green bell pepper, chopped
2 stalks celery, chopped
4 cloves garlic, minced
1½ teaspoons oregano
1½ teaspoons basil
½ teaspoon cinnamon
1 teaspoon sea salt
Pepper to taste
1 quart canned tomatoes or 10 fresh toma-
     toes, chopped
⅓ cup red wine
2 cups firm tofu, drained for 10 minutes,
     pressed and cut into ½-inch cubes
1 large carrot, chopped
2 medium potatoes, chopped
¾ cup broccoli, stems chopped, flowers whole
2 medium zucchini, chopped
Vegetable broth to thin soup

In a large kettle, heat the oil over medium heat; add the onions, pepper, celery, and garlic and sauté until the vegetables are soft and onions transparent. Add the spices; stir-fry for 3 minutes. Mix in the tomatoes, cover, and simmer for 20 minutes. Stir in the wine and tofu; simmer for 1 hour.

30 minutes before serving, add the carrots and potatoes; 10 minutes later add the broccoli. Add the zucchini 10 minutes after the broccoli. Adjust seasoning, adding vegetable broth to dilute if necessary. Ladle into bowls and garnish with croutons and parmesan cheese if desired.

Lentil Soup

Serves 8

3 tablespoons cold-pressed soy or olive oil
3 onions, chopped
5 cloves garlic, minced
3 stalks celery, chopped
1½ teaspoons basil
1 teaspoon oregano
1 teaspoon marjoram
½ teaspoon cinnamon
1 quart canned tomatoes
½ to ¾ cup red wine
1 pound firm tofu, drained for 20 minutes,
    pressed for 30 minutes and cut into ½-inch
    cubes
2 cups lentils
½ to ¾ cup shoyu (natural soy sauce)
8 to 10 cups water or bean or vegetable stock,
    or 4 to 5 cups water plus 4 to 5 cups stock
3 teaspoons vegetable bouillon (if using water
    instead of stock)
3 potatoes, diced
4 to 5 carrots, cut into ¼-inch rounds

In a large kettle, heat the oil over medium heat until lightly hazy; add the onions, garlic and celery and sauté until transparent. Add the spices and stir-fry for 3 to 4 minutes. Add the tomatoes and wine and simmer over low heat for 20 minutes. Mix in the tofu, lentils, shoyu, water and bouillon; cover and simmer for 2 hours, stirring occasionally.

30 minutes before serving, add the potatoes and carrots. Adjust seasoning just before serving; add more water or stock if necessary.

Minestrone Soup

Serves 8 to 10

3 tablespoons cold-pressed olive oil

3 medium onions, chopped

3 cloves garlic, minced

1½ teaspoons basil

1 teaspoon oregano

2 bay leaves

½ teaspoon cinnamon

1 teaspoon sea salt

Dash of black pepper

Dash of cayenne (red) pepper

1 quart canned tomatoes

⅓ to ½ cup red wine

1 pound firm tofu, drained for 20 minutes,
pressed for 20 minutes and cut into 1-inch
cubes

1 large potato, diced

2 medium carrots, diced

2 cups cooked garbanzo beans (chick-peas),
including juice

2 small zucchini, diced

1 cup green peas, preferably fresh

1 cup whole wheat or soy noodles, spirals or
elbows

In a large kettle, heat the oil over medium heat; add the onions and garlic
and sauté until onions are transparent. Add the spices and stir-fry for 3 to
4 minutes. Add the tomatoes, wine and tofu; cover and simmer for 45
minutes to 1 hour. 30 minutes before serving, add the potatoes, carrots,
and garbanzo beans; 15 minutes later add the zucchini, peas and noodles.
Adjust seasoning and dilute with water or stock if desired.

Cream of Mushroom Soup

Serves 6

¾ pound mushrooms
1 small white onion, minced
5 tablespoons butter
1½ cups boiling bean or vegetable stock
3 tablespoons whole wheat or unbleached
    white flour
⅛ teaspoon thyme
2 tablespoons fresh parsley, minced
½ pound firm tofu, drained for 15 minutes,
    pressed for 15 minutes and cut into ½-inch
    cubes
2 cups rich soymilk or 1 cup dairy milk + 1 cup
    cream
1 tablespoon lemon juice
Sea salt and pepper to taste
3 tablespoons sour cream (optional)

Remove the stems from mushrooms; slice the caps and chop stems fine. In a heavy saucepan, sauté the stems and onion in 3 tablespoons of the butter until tender but not brown. Drain through a strainer held over a bowl, pressing down with the back of a wooden spoon to extract all the juice. Pour 3 tablespoons of the stock into a blender; add the onion-mushroom mixture and purée at high speed for 2 to 3 minutes. Set aside.

Return the juice from the mushroom and onions to the saucepan and place over medium-high heat. Sprinkle the flour over the juice and stir briskly with a wire whisk or fork until thickened. Slowly add the remaining stock, stirring until smooth and thick. Add the mushroom-onion purée, thyme, parsley, tofu, and milk; reduce heat and simmer.

Melt the remaining 2 tablespoons of butter in a heavy skillet; add the mushroom caps and sauté over low heat until coated with butter. Add the lemon juice, cover, and simmer for 3 minutes.

Beat the hot soup lightly with a wire whisk; season to taste and add the sautéed mushroom caps. Just before serving, beat in the sour cream if desired.

Cream of Leek Soup

Serves 6 to 8

6 medium leeks
2 tablespoons butter
3 medium onions, finely chopped
6 cups stock (such as a rich vegetable stock)
1 pound potatoes, unpeeled, cut into ½-inch
    cubes
1 cup dry white wine
½ teaspoon pepper
1½ pounds firm tofu, drained for 10 minutes,
    pressed, and cut into ½-inch cubes
1 cup rich soymilk or heavy cream
2 tablespoons fresh parsley, finely chopped
2 tablespoons chives, finely chopped
Sea salt to taste

Wash the leeks well and pat dry. Discard the tough green leaves and chop the more tender greens very fine; slice the white part into rounds.

In a 3-quart pot, melt the butter over medium heat. Add the leek rounds and chopped onions and sauté until soft and translucent. Stir in the leek greens, cover, and cook for 2 to 3 minutes. Add the stock, potatoes and wine and bring to a boil. Reduce heat, cover partially, and simmer for 1 hour.

In a blender or food mill, purée the soup at medium-high speed for 3 minutes; return to the pot. Stir in the pepper and tofu and simmer over low heat for 3 to 4 minutes. Blend in the soymilk or cream, parsley, and chives. Adjust seasoning and serve.

French Onion Soup

Serves 6 to 8
3 tablespoons butter
1 tablespoon cold-pressed soy oil
5 cups yellow onions, thinly sliced
1 teaspoon sea salt
¼ teaspoon date or turbinado sugar (to brown
  the onions)
1 pound firm tofu, crumbled
3 tablespoons whole wheat flour
2 quarts boiling brown stock (the liquid from
  cooking pinto, kidney, or black beans) or
  1 quart boiling water + 1 quart stock
½ cup red wine
Sea salt and pepper to taste

In a heavy 4-quart kettle, heat the butter and oil over low heat; add the
onions and cook, covered, for 15 minutes, stirring occasionally. Increase
the heat to medium and stir in the salt and sugar; add the crumbled tofu
and cook for 30 to 40 minutes or until the onions have turned an even
golden brown, stirring often. Sprinkle in the flour and stir for 3 minutes.

Remove the soup from heat and blend in the boiling liquid. Add the
wine and seasoning to taste. Simmer, partially covered, for 30 to 40
minutes occasionally skimming the foam off the top. Adjust seasoning
and serve immediately.

Black Bean Soup

Serves 8

2 cups black beans, picked over, washed and
  drained
8 cups cold water
3 tablespoons cold-pressed olive oil
1 pound firm tofu, crumbled
3 medium onions, chopped
3 stalks celery, chopped
2 bay leaves
2 tablespoons fresh parsley, chopped
½ teaspoon sea salt
⅛ teaspoon black pepper
½ teaspoon savory
⅔ cup dry sherry
2 hard-boiled eggs, sliced
2 lemons, sliced

Place the beans in a soup kettle with cold water to cover and allow to soak overnight.

Drain the beans, return to the kettle and add the 8 cups of water; simmer over low heat until soft. In a skillet, heat the oil over medium heat; add the crumbled tofu, onions and celery and sauté until the tofu is golden and vegetables are transparent. Add to the beans. Stir in the bay leaves, parsley, salt, pepper and savory and simmer, covered, over medium-low heat for 1½ hours, adding water if the soup becomes too thick.

Pour the soup into a blender and whirl at medium speed for 2 to 3 minutes; return to the pot. Add the sherry and cook over low heat until hot. Adjust seasoning to taste. Ladle the soup into individual serving bowls and garnish with slices of egg and circles of lemon.

Barley Soup

Serves 6

¾ cup pearl barley

3 cups vegetable stock or water

2 medium onions, minced

1 large carrot, minced

6 large mushrooms, thinly sliced

2½ quarts bean stock

1 pound firm tofu, drained for 30 minutes,
    patted dry and cut into 1-inch cubes

Sea salt and pepper to taste

Sour cream (optional)

Parsley to garnish

In a medium-sized saucepan, combine the barley and vegetable stock; bring to a boil over medium heat. Reduce heat and simmer for 1 hour, or until the liquid is absorbed.

In a kettle, combine the onions, carrots and mushrooms with 1 to 2 tablespoons of water; steam over medium heat for 5 minutes, or until the vegetables are softened. Add the bean stock and tofu and bring to a boil. Reduce heat and simmer for 30 minutes. Add the barley and salt and pepper to taste; simmer for 5 minutes. Ladle the soup into heated bowls and garnish each serving with finely chopped parsley and sour cream, if desired. Serve piping hot.

Borscht

Serves 6 to 8
5 large beets with leafy tops
1 large onion
¾ pound firm tofu, drained for 20 minutes,
    pressed for 10 minutes and cut into ½-inch
    cubes
10 cups water or vegetable stock
4 tablespoons vegetable bouillon
1 large potato, cut into ½-inch cubes
8 to 10 tablespoons fresh lemon juice, strained
½ to 1 tablespoon honey or to taste
Sea salt to taste
Sour cream

Wash and chop the tender beet leaves, discarding the stems and tough leaves. Coarsely grate the beets and onions. Combine the leaves, beets, and onion in a large kettle; add the tofu, water, and bouillon. Bring to a boil; reduce heat, cover and simmer for 20 minutes. Add the potato and cook for 20 minutes more. Remove the soup from heat and add 6 tablespoons of lemon juice and the honey; chill thoroughly. Adjust seasoning, adding salt, lemon juice and honey as needed. Soup will keep for up to 1 week if refrigerated and covered. Add a spoonful of sour cream to each bowl just before serving.

Puréed Vegetable Soup with Tofu

Serves 6 to 8

2 quarts bean or vegetable stock

2 pounds firm tofu, drained for 15 minutes,
     pressed and cut into 1-inch cubes

2 ears corn, cut into 1-inch rounds

1 large onion, quartered

1 large tomato, quartered

1 green bell pepper, quartered and seeded

2 cloves garlic, peeled

¼ cup coriander leaves, chopped

½ pound fresh pumpkin, peeled and cut into
     2-inch pieces, or ½ pound yellow squash,
     cut into small pieces

2 to 3 tablespoons red wine (optional)

1 cup canned tomatoes

2 teaspoons sea salt

¼ teaspoon black pepper

1 teaspoon basil

2 ounces vermicelli or rice

In a 4-quart kettle, combine the first 10 ingredients and bring to a boil over high heat. Reduce heat, cover, and simmer for 1 hour.

Remove the tofu with a slotted spoon and set aside. Using a slotted spoon, transfer the onion, tomato, green pepper, garlic, coriander and pumpkin to a blender. Add ¾ cup of the cooking broth and purée at high speed for ½ minute. Return to the kettle. Stir in the tofu, tomatoes, and spices and bring to a boil over high heat. Add the vermicelli or rice; reduce to medium heat and cook for 10 minutes for vermicelli, 20 minutes for rice, or until tender. Adjust seasoning. Serve hot.

Corn Chowder

Serves 6 to 8

2 cups corn kernels
2 to 3 tablespoons cold-pressed soy oil
1 cup regular tofu, reshaped and cut into tiny
    bits
4 medium onions, cut crosswise into ⅛-inch-
    thick slices
3 medium boiling potatoes, unpeeled, diced
    into ¼-inch pieces
2 cups vegetable stock or water
2 cups rich soymilk or 1 cup milk + 1 cup light
    cream
1 teaspoon marjoram
Sea salt and pepper to taste

Place 1 cup of the corn in a blender and blend at high speed for 30 seconds. Turn off the blender, scrape down the sides with a spatula, and blend again until the corn is a smooth purée. Set aside.

In a heavy 4-quart casserole, heat the oil over medium heat; add the tofu bits and sauté until crisp and brown. Remove from pan and drain on paper toweling. Add the onions to the oil and sauté for 10 minutes, stirring often, until soft and golden. Do not burn. Stir in the corn purée, the remaining cup of corn kernels, potatoes and water; bring to a boil over high heat. Reduce heat and simmer, partially covered, until the potatoes are tender. Add the soymilk and simmer lightly for 5 minutes, stirring constantly, until heated through. Stir in the tofu bits; adjust seasoning to taste. Serve immediately.

Split Pea Soup with Thick Agé

Serves 6
1½ cups yellow or green split peas, washed well
2 quarts bean or vegetable stock
1 onion, chopped
1 stalk celery, diced
2 carrots, chopped
2 cloves garlic, minced
1 bay leaf
1 teaspoon marjoram
½ teaspoon thyme
1 teaspoon fresh parsley, minced
Sea salt and pepper to taste
2 to 3 tablespoons red wine
Two 5-ounce cakes frozen thick agé, reconsti-
    tuted, broiled and sliced into strips
1 to 2 tablespoons soy margarine or butter
15 to 20 small mushrooms

In a heavy soup pot, combine the peas, stock, onion, celery, carrots and spices; bring to a boil. Pour in the wine and cover the pot with a tight fitting lid. Cook for 2 hours over medium heat, stirring occasionally. Adjust seasoning to taste.

Place half of the soup in a blender and purée at medium speed for 2 to 3 minutes until smooth, diluting with rich soymilk or broth if necessary. Return the soup to the pot; add the broiled agé strips and allow to stand for several hours or overnight in the refrigerator for the flavors to blend.

Just before reheating the soup, sauté the whole mushrooms lightly in the margarine or butter; add to the soup and heat slowly until piping hot. Adjust seasoning to taste. Thin soup with rich soymilk or broth, if desired. Serve hot with bread and a bowl of brown rice.

Tofu, Chick-Pea and
Green Chili Soup

Serves 6

1 cup dried chick-peas (garbanzo beans)
2 quarts water
Cold-pressed soy oil for sautéing
2 pounds regular tofu, reshaped and cut into
    1-inch cubes
Dash of shoyu (natural soy sauce)
2 medium onions, coarsely chopped
1 bay leaf, crumbled
1 tablespoon sea salt
8 whole black peppercorns
6 tablespoons uncooked long grain brown rice
1½ teaspoons dried oregano, crumbled
3 tablespoons Ortega chilies, finely chopped
½ pound Monterey Jack cheese, cut into
    ¼-inch pieces
2 tablespoons fresh parsley, finely chopped
1 large firm ripe avocado, halved, peeled and
    cut lengthwise into thin slices

Wash and pick over the chick-peas; place in a large bowl with water to cover. Soak at room temperature for at least 12 hours.

Drain the chick-peas and place in a heavy 4-quart casserole with 2 quarts of water; bring to a boil over high heat. Reduce heat and simmer, partially covered, for 1 hour or until tender. With a slotted spoon, transfer the chick-peas to a bowl and set aside, reserving the cooking water.

In a large skillet, heat enough oil to densely cover the bottom; add the tofu and sauté over high heat. Sprinkle the tofu with shoyu and remove from heat; add to the chick-pea water. Mix in the onions, bay leaf, sea salt and peppercorns. Add more water or vegetable stock as needed to completely cover the tofu. Bring soup to a boil; reduce heat and simmer, uncovered, for 1 hour. Cover, turn off heat, and allow to stand for one hour so that the flavors permeate the tofu.

Remove the tofu with a slotted spoon; strain the stock. Return the stock and the tofu to the pot and bring to a boil. Stir in the rice, oregano, and chilies. Reduce heat, cover, and simmer for 20 minutes, or until the rice is tender. Stir in the chick-peas and simmer for 10 minutes more. Adjust seasoning to taste. Ladle soup into a large serving bowl and sprinkle with diced cheese and parsley. Arrange the avocado slices on top and serve immediately with steamed tortillas or chunks of bread.

Peanut Soup

Serves 5 to 6
3 cups dark bean stock
1 medium onion, coarsely chopped
1 large leek, trimmed and coarsely chopped
2 medium carrots, sliced into ½-inch rounds
¼ cup uncooked long grain brown rice
One 1-inch piece dried hot red chili
½ teaspoon sea salt
Cold-pressed soy oil for deep-frying
1½ pounds regular tofu, reshaped and cut into
    french-fry-sized strips
½ cup smooth natural peanut butter (unhy-
    drogenated)

In a heavy 3-quart kettle, combine the stock, onion, leek and carrots; bring to a boil over high heat. Reduce heat and simmer, partially covered, for 30 minutes. Place the soup in a blender and purée until smooth; return to the pot and bring to a boil. Add the rice, chili and salt; reduce heat, cover, and simmer for 20 minutes.

In a wok or heavy skillet, heat 3 inches of soy oil to 350°F. on a deep-fry or candy thermometer. Fry the tofu pieces, 3 at a time, until golden brown. Remove with a slotted spoon and drain on paper toweling.

When the rice is tender, remove ½ cup of the soup and mix with the peanut butter in a small bowl until smooth. Stir the peanut butter mixture into the soup; cover and simmer for 5 minutes. Remove and discard the chili; adjust seasoning to taste. Place 2 or 3 of the tofu strips in each bowl; pour soup on top and serve immediately.

Salads

Indonesian Vegetable Salad

Serves 8
½ pound fresh bean sprouts, steamed for 1
    minute
½ pound green cabbage, shredded
1 cucumber, thinly sliced
1 bunch radishes, thinly sliced
3½ pounds firm tofu, drained, pressed and cut
    into 1-inch cubes
1 cup unsalted, roasted peanuts, chopped

Dressing:
3 hot fresh chilies, minced
1 clove garlic, finely chopped
½ teaspoon fresh ginger, minced
¼ cup vinegar
2 tablespoons date or raw sugar or 1 table-
    spoon honey
2 cups water
Sea salt and pepper to taste

Arrange the bean sprouts, cabbage, cucumber, radishes and tofu in a mound on a large platter.

In a blender, combine the chilies, garlic, ginger, vinegar, and sugar or honey and mix well at medium speed for 1 to 2 minutes, stopping when necessary to scrape down the sides with a spatula. Add the water and blend for 2 minutes more. Adjust seasoning. Pour the dressing over the vegetables and garnish with the peanuts. Serve at once.

Tofu Louis

Serves 6

1½ cups homemade mayonnaise (or honey-
sweetened)

¼ cup ketchup (*Hain*-brand honey-sweetened)

3 tablespoons scallions, finely chopped

3 tablespoons green peppers, finely chopped

1 tablespoon fresh lemon juice, strained

1½ teaspoons A-1 sauce (an all-natural
product)

4 drops Tobasco sauce (an all-natural
product)

½ teaspoon sea salt

1½ pounds firm tofu, drained for 10 minutes,
pressed for ½ hour and cut into ½-inch
cubes

3 large avocados

1 head Boston lettuce (or red-leaf lettuce)

2 medium-sized firm, ripe tomatoes, each cut
into 6 wedges

3 hard-boiled eggs, quartered

In a medium-sized bowl, combine the first 8 ingredients and mix with a wire whisk. Adjust seasoning to taste. Add the tofu and toss gently. Refrigerate for 3 to 4 hours.

Cut each avocado in half; remove the pit and fill each half with the chilled mixture. Place the avocado halves on a plate. Surround with lettuce and garnish with eggs and tomatoes.

Tofu and Sweet Red Pepper Salad

Serves 2 to 3

4 large sweet red peppers
1 head lettuce, torn into bite-sized pieces
1 bunch green onions, finely sliced
½ cup celery, diced
4 ounces regular tofu, reshaped and cut into
     1-inch cubes

Vinaigrette Dressing:
2 tablespoons apple cider or red wine vinegar
2 teaspoons Dijon-style mustard (with no
     chemicals or preservatives)
¼ teaspoon sea salt
⅛ teaspoon black pepper
6 tablespoons olive oil

Place the peppers over a flame and roast until blackened and blistered on all sides; cool. Peel the peppers under cold running water; cut lengthwise into ¼-inch slices, discarding the seeds and white membrane.

In a large salad bowl, toss the lettuce with onions and celery; arrange the tofu and pepper slices on top.

In a small mixing bowl, combine the first 4 dressing ingredients; gradually add the oil, whisking constantly until thoroughly blended. Toss with the salad just before serving.

Tofu-Spinach Salad

Serves 3

1 large bunch fresh spinach leaves, torn into
    bite-sized pieces

½ pound firm tofu, drained, pressed for 20
    minutes and cut into 1-inch cubes

½ cup raw mushrooms, sliced

½ cup croutons

Oil and vinegar dressing with honey and 1
    hard-boiled egg, diced

In a medium-sized bowl, toss the spinach leaves, tofu, mushrooms and croutons. Prepare your favorite oil and vinegar dressing, adding a small amount of honey and 1 hard-boiled egg. Blend well; toss with salad and serve.

Tomato-Tofu Salad

Serves 4

4 large ripe tomatoes, cut into ½-inch-thick
    slices

1 red onion, thinly sliced

½ pound firm tofu, drained for 20 minutes,
    pressed for 30 minutes and cut into small
    bits

Dash of salt and pepper

3 cloves garlic, minced

¼ cup parsley, minced

1 teaspoon basil

1½ teaspoons cold-pressed soy, sesame or
    olive oil

1 to 2 tablespoons red wine vinegar

In a large rectangular dish, place a layer of tomatoes; top with a layer of onions, and one of tofu. Sprinkle with salt, pepper, garlic, parsley, basil, oil, and vinegar. Continue layering until all the ingredients are used. Refrigerate for 3 to 4 hours, or until well chilled.

Tofu Egyptian Salad

Serves 4
1 large cucumber, peeled, halved lengthwise
    and seeded
Sprinkle of sea salt
12 ounces firm tofu, crumbled
½ cup mild onion, finely chopped
¼ cup fresh lemon juice
2 to 3 tablespoons cold-pressed olive oil
Freshly ground pepper to taste
Mint sprigs to garnish

Score the cucumber with the tines of a fork; sprinkle with salt and allow to stand for 20 minutes.

In a medium-sized bowl, combine the tofu, onion, lemon juice, and oil; season with pepper and sea salt to taste. Drain, rinse and slice the cucumber. Add to the tofu mixture. Place salad in a shallow serving dish and decorate with mint sprigs. Chill for 1 hour before serving.

Stuffed Tomatoes

Serves 4 to 6
4 large, firm, ripe tomatoes or 6 medium-sized
    ones
½ pound regular tofu, drained for 10 minutes
    and patted dry
⅓ cup homemade or honey-sweetened
    mayonnaise
3 tablespoons Dijon-style mustard
⅓ cup sweet pickle, chopped
1 teaspoon sea salt
½ teaspoon bell pepper, minced
½ teaspoon paprika
1 stalk celery, chopped
2 whole green onions, sliced
1 carrot, shredded

Cut stem tops 1½ inches in diameter off the tomatoes. With a teaspoon, hollow out the inside of each tomato. Sprinkle the inside with salt; turn upside down on paper towels and allow to drain for 20 to 30 minutes.

In a medium-sized bowl, mash the tofu with a wooden spoon; add the mayonnaise and blend well. Mix in the remaining ingredients; adjust seasoning to taste. With a teaspoon, fill the hollow tomatoes with the tofu mixture. Garnish with paprika and refrigerate until ready to serve.

The tofu mixture also may be used as a stuffing for other vegetables, as a spread on crackers, or as a sandwich filling on heavy dark bread, garnished with sliced onions and tomatoes, and lettuce or sprouts.

Bean and Tofu Vegetable Salad

Serves 3 to 4

1 cup cooked garbanzo beans (chick-peas)
1 cup cooked kidney beans
1 cup raw cauliflower, flowers separated and
    sliced
2 small zucchini, sliced
1 small onion, thinly sliced
½ pound firm tofu, drained for 20 minutes,
    pressed for 1 hour and cut into 2-inch
    slivers

Italian herb dressing:
6 tablespoons cold-pressed olive oil
¼ cup red wine vinegar
1 clove garlic, minced
¾ teaspoon sea salt or to taste
¼ teaspoon honey
¼ teaspoon oregano
¼ teaspoon basil
¼ teaspoon black pepper

In a medium-sized bowl, combine all the salad ingredients. Mix the dressing ingredients together in a jar and shake well. Toss lightly with the salad. Cover and refrigerate for 1 to 3 hours before serving.

Greek Spinach-Tofu Salad

Serves 4 to 6

1 large bunch spinach, trimmed, rinsed and
    torn into bite-sized pieces
3 green onions, thinly sliced
1 small cucumber, sliced
½ pound firm tofu, drained for 30 minutes,
    pressed for 30 minutes and cut into 2-inch
    strips, ½ inch wide
1 hard-boiled egg, sliced
6 cherry tomatoes, cut into halves
10 medium mushrooms, sliced
Black olives to garnish
2 tablespoons cold-pressed olive oil
4 tablespoons fresh lemon juice, strained
½ teaspoon basil
½ teaspoon dry mustard
Wine vinegar to taste

In a large serving bowl, combine the spinach, onions and cucumber;
arrange rows of tofu, egg, tomatoes, and mushrooms on top. Garnish
with black olives.

Combine the oil, lemon juice, basil, and mustard; stir well, adding wine
vinegar to taste. Sprinkle dressing over the salad just before serving.

Marinated Tofu-Pepper Salad

Serves 6

3 large green bell peppers
1½ pounds regular tofu, reshaped and sliced
   into long strips
¾ teaspoon sea salt
½ teaspoon black pepper
1 small onion, finely chopped
1 teaspoon oregano
4 tablespoons cold-pressed olive oil
4 tablespoons cold-pressed soy oil
4 tablespoons wine vinegar
Pimento strips and sliced black olives to garnish

Wash the peppers and roast over an open flame or bake in a preheated 450°F. oven until wilted and the skins are blistered. Cool. Peel the peppers under cold running water and cut into narrow strips, discarding the seeds and white membranes.

Place the pepper strips and tofu in a mixing bowl; sprinkle with salt, pepper, onion, oregano, oils, and vinegar. Toss lightly and refrigerate overnight. Garnish with olives and pimento. Serve at room temperature.

Tunisian Mixed Salad

Serves 6
2 medium-sized bell peppers
1 cup onion, minced
2 medium tomatoes, seeded and diced
2 large McIntosh apples, cored and diced
1 teaspoon hot green chili pepper, minced
   (such as jalapeños)
8 ounces regular tofu, reshaped and cut into
   1-inch cubes
¼ to ⅓ cup cold-pressed olive oil
2 tablespoons cider vinegar
1 tablespoon crushed dried mint leaves or
   2 tablespoons fresh mint
Sea salt and freshly ground pepper to taste

Place the peppers over a flame and roast until blackened and blistered on all sides; cool. Peel the peppers under cold running water; cut in half and dice, discarding the seeds and white membranes.

In a serving bowl, combine the peppers, onion, tomatoes, apples, chili pepper and tofu; add the oil and vinegar, mixing well. Sprinkle with mint, salt and pepper. Serve in scoops with wedges of warmed pita bread.

Rice Salad with Marinated Vegetables

Serves 6 to 8

1 cup zucchini, sliced
½ cup green beans, coarsely chopped
½ cup crookneck squash, sliced
½ cup carrots, sliced
¼ cup water

Vinaigrette Dressing:
⅓ cup cold-pressed olive or soy oil
⅛ cup cider or red wine vinegar
¼ teaspoon dry mustard
¼ teaspoon sea salt
Dash of freshly ground pepper
Dash of freshly snipped dill

½ cup jicama, diced (found in many supermarkets and Latin markets)
2 tablespoons red onion, chopped
4 cups cooked brown rice, chilled
1¾ cups sour cream
¾ cup regular tofu, whirled in a blender until
   smooth
Juice of ½ lemon
2 cloves garlic, minced
Sea salt and pepper to taste
Chips or wedges of pita bread

Place the zucchini, green beans, squash, carrots and water in a large saucepan; parboil over medium heat for 5 minutes. Drain and place in a large mixing bowl to cool. In a small bowl, combine all the dressing ingredients; blend thoroughly. Add the jicama, onion and dressing to the vegetables; toss, cover, and refrigerate overnight.

In a large bowl, combine the rice, sour cream, tofu, lemon juice and garlic; mix well. Add salt and pepper to taste. Arrange the mixture in a ring on a large serving platter.

Just before serving, place the chilled vegetables in the center of the rice mold and surround with chips or pita bread.

Artichoke Hearts Polita

Serves 6

1 medium-sized carrots, thinly sliced
2 large onions, coarsely chopped
3 large potatoes, unpeeled and quartered
4 whole green onions, finely chopped
½ teaspoon sea salt
⅛ teaspoon pepper
½ tablespoon dried dill or 1 tablespoon fresh
    dill
Pinch of date or raw sugar or ¼ teaspoon
    honey
½ cup cold-pressed olive oil
3 tablespoons fresh lemon juice, strained
2 tablespoons whole wheat or unbleached
    white flour
One 9-ounce package frozen artichoke hearts,
    thawed
8 ounces firm tofu, crumbled

Place the carrot, onions, potatoes, green onions, salt, pepper, dill and sugar in a large saucepan; add water to cover and bring to a boil. Reduce heat, cover, and simmer for 15 minutes.

In a small bowl, beat the olive oil, lemon juice, and flour with a wire whisk until well blended. Pour over the vegetables and simmer, covered, for 7 minutes or until the sauce thickens slightly. Add the artichoke hearts and crumbled tofu and bring to a boil. Reduce heat, cover, and simmer for 8 minutes or until the vegetables are tender. Allow to cool. Adjust seasoning to taste. Serve slightly chilled.

Potato Salad

Serves 8 to 10

4 ounces regular tofu, whirled in a blender until
  smooth
¾ cup homemade or honey-sweetened
  mayonnaise
½ teaspoon sea salt
1 tablespoon lemon juice
½ teaspoon dry mustard
½ teaspoon pepper
2 hard-boiled eggs, chopped (optional)
6 cups steamed potatoes, unpeeled and cubed
1 cup celery, chopped
½ cup green pepper, diced
½ cup onion, finely chopped
Boston or red-leaf lettuce leaves to garnish
1 hard-boiled egg, sliced (optional)
Paprika to garnish
Parsley, minced, to garnish (optional)

In a large mixing bowl, combine the whirled tofu and mayonnaise; add the
next 9 ingredients, mixing well. Adjust seasoning to taste; chill. Serve on
lettuce leaves, garnished with egg slices, paprika and parsley.

Moroccan Eggplant Salad

Serves 4 to 6
2 medium-sized eggplants, peeled
Sprinkle of sea salt
¼ cup cold-pressed olive oil
3 large tomatoes, seeded and chopped
2 green bell peppers, sliced
8 ounces firm tofu, crumbled
2 to 3 cloves garlic, minced
1 tablespoon fresh cilantro or parsley, chopped
1 teaspoon sweet paprika
½ teaspoon ground cumin
Juice of ½ lemon

Cut the eggplant into ½-inch slices; sprinkle with salt and drain in a colander for 15 minutes. Rinse slices well to remove salt and pat dry.

In a large skillet, heat the olive oil over high heat; add the eggplant slices and sauté until golden brown on both sides. (This can also be done in the broiler by brushing the slices lightly with olive oil and browning both sides under the broiler.) Remove from the pan and allow to cool. Reduce heat to medium-low; add the tomatoes and green peppers and cook, covered, for 10 to 15 minutes, stirring occasionally. Mash the vegetables with a wooden spoon. Quarter the eggplant slices and add, stirring well. Cover and cook for 20 to 25 minutes, or until very soft. Add the tofu, garlic, cilantro, paprika and cumin; cook, uncovered, over medium heat, stirring often, for 10 minutes, or until liquid evaporates. Pour off excess oil; season to taste with lemon juice and salt. Serve with wedges of pita bread or sesame crackers.

Tabouli

Serves 6 to 8

2 cups water
1 cup dry bulghur or cracked wheat
1 pound firm tofu, crumbled
1 large tomato, chopped
1 bunch whole green onions, sliced
1 to 2 teaspoons sea salt
½ teaspoon black pepper
1 cup parsley, finely chopped
½ to 1 cup fresh mint, finely chopped
3 tablespoons fresh lemon juice, strained
¼ cup cold-pressed olive oil

In a large serving bowl, combine the water and bulghur; allow to stand for 1 to 2 hours, or until all the water is absorbed and the grain is tender.

Add the tofu, tomatoes, and onions to the bulghur; season with salt and pepper. Sprinkle the salad with parsley, mint and lemon juice; pour in the olive oil. Toss lightly with a wooden spoon. Adjust seasoning to taste. Serve with wedges of pita bread.

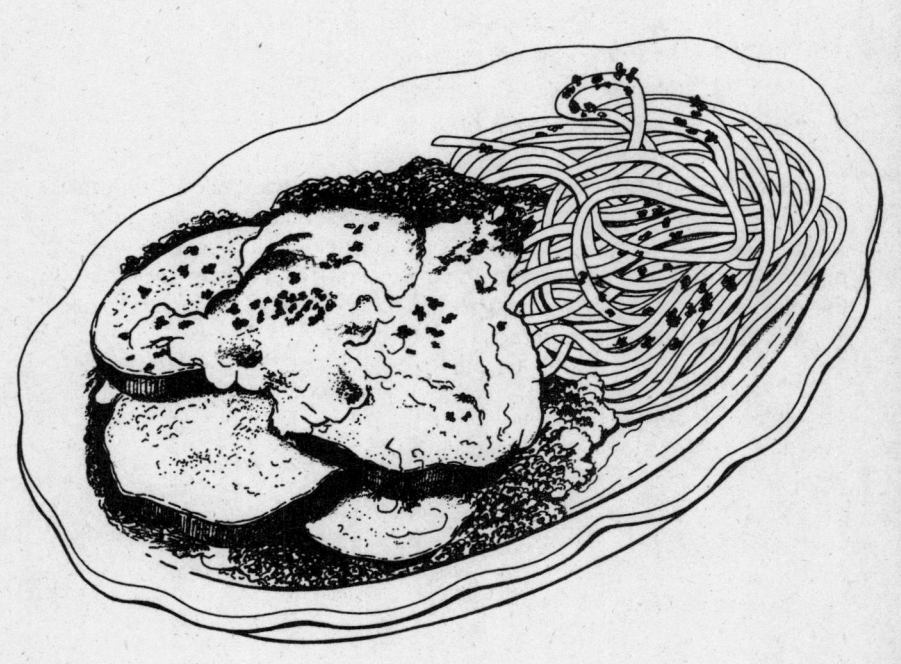

Entrées

Eggplant Parmesan

Serves 4 to 5
2 medium-sized eggplants
¼ to ½ teaspoon olive oil for each slice of
   eggplant
Sprinkle of sea salt and black pepper
Spaghetti sauce (see Lasagne) or other Italian
   sauce
Tofu filling (see Lasagne)
Sliced mushrooms to garnish (optional)

Slice the eggplant into ½- to 1-inch slices, with peel on; place slices in a shallow pan. Brush with the olive oil and sprinkle with salt and pepper. Broil for 3 to 4 minutes or until light brown; turn the slices over and broil until brown. Remove from broiler and allow to cool.

Preheat oven to 350° F. In a 3-quart casserole, spoon sauce to cover the bottom; alternate layers of eggplant slices, tofu filling, and sauce, finishing with a layer of tofu on the top. Garnish with sliced mushrooms if desired. Bake for 30 minutes. Allow eggplant to stand for 10 minutes before serving. This dish is delicious served with hot buttered noodles and bread.

Spicy Ganmo Balls

Makes 2½ dozen

2 pounds regular tofu, drained for 20 minutes
and squeezed

3 cloves garlic, minced

4 whole green onions, sliced

1 teaspoon anise or fennel seeds

¼ cup fresh parsley, snipped

1¼ teaspoons sea salt

3 dashes black pepper

½ cup grated Parmesan or Romano cheese
(optional)

1 egg, beaten

½ cup dry whole wheat bread crumbs, finely
ground

2 to 3 tablespoons olive oil

Spaghetti sauce (see Lasagne) or other Italian
sauce

In a large bowl, knead the tofu for 5 minutes; add the spices and cheese and knead for 3 minutes more, or until the mixture is smooth and doughy. Add the beaten egg, stirring well. Roll teaspoonfuls of the mixture between wetted palms of the hands to form walnut-sized balls; roll the balls in the bread crumbs.

In a heavy 10-inch skillet, heat the oil over medium heat. Fry the balls, 3 or 4 at a time, turning frequently until golden brown. Drain on paper towels or newspaper for two minutes. Combine the tofu balls and the spaghetti sauce in a large saucepan; heat through and simmer over low heat for up to one hour, as desired. Flavor improves with cooking time. Serve over spaghetti noodles.

VARIATIONS: Make balls as directed and use as sandwich filling for pita bread.

Make balls as directed, flattening the dough between the palms rather than rolling. Use on sprouted wheat buns with sandwich trimmings and a slice of cheese melted on each patty.

Chili Con Tofu

Chili seems to have become an almost national dish and certainly an all-American favorite.

Serves 6 to 8

3 tablespoons cold-pressed olive oil
3 medium onions, chopped
2 stalks celery, chopped
4 cloves garlic, minced
1½ pounds firm tofu, crumbled
1 teaspoon basil
1 teaspoon oregano
2 to 4 tablespoons chili powder
1 teaspoon ground cuminos
1 quart canned tomatoes or 8 medium, fresh
   tomatoes
1 15-ounce can tomato sauce
4 cups cooked pinto beans or a combination of
   pinto, kidney and black beans
Freshly ground black pepper to taste
1 teaspoon sea salt

In a large kettle, heat the oil over medium heat; add the onions, celery, garlic and tofu and sauté until onions are transparent. Add the spices and sauté, stirring well; mix in the tomatoes, including juice if canned; if fresh, chop before adding so they will juice. Cook, uncovered, for 15 minutes. Add the tomato sauce and the beans. Reduce heat, cover, and simmer for 1 hour, stirring occasionally. Adjust seasoning. Serve hot, with a pat of butter on each serving. Accompany with a green salad and steaming corn bread.

Mattar Panir

This is a mild curry, with a refreshing enjoyable flavor.

Serves 4
12 ounces firm tofu
Cold-pressed soy or peanut oil for deep-frying
2 tablespoons fresh ginger, finely chopped
2 teaspoons jalapeño chilies, minced
1 onion, chopped
3 tablespoons tomato paste or heavy tomato
    purée
1 teaspoon turmeric
¼ teaspoon cayenne pepper
1½ teaspoons sea salt
2 tablespoons sour cream or unflavored
    yoghurt
1¾ cups water or whey from homemade tofu
2½ cups fresh shelled peas (or two 10-ounce
    packages frozen peas, thoroughly
    defrosted)
1½ tablespoons Garam Masala (recipe follows)

Drain the tofu in a colander for 30 minutes; slice crosswise into ¾-inch-thick slices. Press the slices for 30 minutes between two towels; cut into cubes.

Pour 1 inch of oil into a large heavy frying pan; heat to 350° F. on a deep-fry or candy thermometer. Fry the tofu cubes, 4 or 5 at a time, turning frequently until browned on all sides, for 2 to 3 minutes. Remove and drain on paper towels or newspaper; cool, cover, and chill if prepared in advance.

Pour off all except ¼ cup of the oil; add the ginger, chilies, and onion and sauté over medium heat until onions are limp, stirring constantly. Add the tomato paste or purée, turmeric and cayenne; reduce heat and cook for 8 to 10 minutes until onions are very soft. Mix in the salt, sour cream, and water. Cool, cover, and chill if prepared in advance.

To serve: Add the tofu cubes to the heated sauce and simmer, covered, over low heat for 5 minutes. Add the peas; simmer, uncovered, until peas are tender, 10 to 15 minutes for fresh peas, 5 minutes for frozen. Pour into a serving dish and sprinkle with garam masala. Serve with sliced cucumbers and onions in yoghurt, sliced tomatoes, and steamed brown rice.

Garam Masala:

This is a mild and fragrant spice with a delicious, unusual flavor, useful in adjusting the seasoning of any dish.

Makes ⅓ cup
3 tablespoons coriander seed
2 teaspoons cumin seed
8 whole cloves
1 stick cinnamon, 2 inches long
½ teaspoon whole black pepper
4 bay leaves

Place the coriander seed and cumin seed in a dry frying pan over medium heat and roast, shaking often, for 4 minutes, or until seeds are lightly browned. Place the seeds in a blender or nut grinder with the remaining ingredients and grind to a fine powder. Store in an airtight container.

Enchiladas

This tofu adaptation of Mexican Cheese Enchiladas is one of my favorite recipes.

Serves 8

Salsa:

2 tablespoons cold-pressed soy oil
1 onion, chopped
2 cloves garlic, minced
⅓ cup green chilies, diced (fresh jalapeño or
　　Ortega brand canned)
3 tablespoons chili powder
1 teaspoon cuminos
¼ to ½ teaspoon cayenne (red) pepper
1 teaspoon sea salt
¼ teaspoon black pepper
1 cup tomato sauce
1½ cups tomato paste
3 cups bean stock or water

Filling:

1½ cups regular tofu, drained for 30 minutes
　　and mashed into small curds
½ to ¾ cup sour cream
1 teaspoon sea salt
½ teaspoon turmeric
Dash of pepper
¼ teaspoon paprika
½ cup mushrooms, sliced
½ cup whole green onions, sliced

12 to 15 medium-sized flour tortillas (prefer-
　　ably whole wheat)
Cold-pressed soy oil for deep-frying
⅓ cup black olives, sliced or chopped
　　(optional)
Chopped parsley or cilantro to garnish

Salsa: In a 3- or 4-quart heavy pot, heat the oil over medium heat; add the onions and garlic and sauté until onions are soft and transparent. Add the remaining salsa ingredients in the order above, sautéing the spices for 3 to 4 minutes before adding the liquid ingredients. Simmer for 20 minutes. Turn off heat and allow to stand until ready to use.

Filling: In a medium-sized mixing bowl, blend the tofu and sour cream until very smooth; add the spices and beat well. Add the mushrooms and green onions. Chill if prepared in advance.

Preheat oven to 350° F. In a large heavy skillet, heat 1-inch-deep cold-pressed soy oil over medium heat until lightly hazy. Dip the tortillas, one at a time, into the oil until they puff slightly, but don't cook (they must be soft); turn over with a pair of tongs and remove after 5 seconds. Immediately dip each tortilla into the salsa to form a thin film, or place the tortilla on a plate and spoon the salsa over it, lightly coating each side. Place the tortilla flat on a plate and spoon 1 to 2 tablespoons filling into the center. Fold the top and bottom of the tortilla toward the center and fold over one side to cover the filling. Push the filling in snugly against the tortilla and roll it once or twice to form a closed cylinder. Prepare all the tortillas, using two-thirds of the filling.

Spoon enough salsa into two 13″ × 15″ pans to lightly cover the bottoms. Place the enchiladas, seam down and side-by-side, in the pans; spoon salsa over the tops and use the remaining filling to decorate each one with a thin strip of filling on top. Garnish with chopped or sliced black olives. Bake for 25 to 35 minutes, or until heated through. Sprinkle tops with chopped cilantro or parsley if desired. Serve immediately. Accompany with refried beans and tossed green salad for a hearty, complete meal.

VARIATIONS: Add cooked rice or another grain to the filling for a more varied taste and a complete protein.

Prepare a Roasted Nut Loaf and add, cooked, to the filling, or sprinkle on top for a special meal.

Savory Tofu Stew

Serves 6 to 8

¼ cup cold-pressed olive oil

1½ cups onion, cut into crescents

1 cup carrots, sliced into ¼-inch rounds

1 cup celery, sliced

2 cloves garlic, minced

1 cup firm tofu, pressed for 10 minutes and cut
  into 1-inch cubes

1½ cups zucchini or summer squash, cut into
  chunks

2 tomatoes, diced

1 tablespoon basil

¼ teaspoon rosemary

¼ teaspoon savory

2 bay leaves

Freshly ground black pepper to taste

2 cups tomato juice

⅓ cup shoyu (natural soy sauce)

In a large kettle, heat the oil over medium heat; add the onions, carrots, celery and garlic and sauté until onions are translucent. Add the tofu, zucchini, and tomatoes, and sauté for 4 minutes. Add the spices, stirring constantly, and cook for 2 minutes or until fragrant. Pour in the tomato juice and shoyu, stirring well; reduce heat and simmer for 1 hour. Serve with fresh buttered biscuits, corn-on-the-cob and a green salad.

Tofu Ratatouille

Ratatouille is a Middle-Eastern/Mediterranean vegetable stew. Unlike many versions, this dish retains the color and texture of each vegetable, and can be served hot or cold, or as a filling for crêpes or omelettes.

Serves 8

1 medium-sized eggplant, unpeeled
1 pound zucchini, unpeeled
1 teaspoon sea salt
6 tablespoons whole wheat or unbleached
   white flour
⅓ to ½ cup cold-pressed olive oil
1 pound firm tofu, drained for 20 minutes,
   pressed for 20 minutes and cut into 1-inch
   cubes
1 large onion, finely chopped
2 green bell peppers, cut into ½-inch strips
2 cloves garlic, minced
2 pounds tomatoes, cut into ½-inch strips
Sea salt and pepper to taste
3 to 6 tablespoons Parmesan cheese, freshly
   grated
6 tablespoons fresh parsley, minced
3 tablespoons fresh dill, snipped
1½ teaspoons basil

Slice the eggplant into ½-inch-thick pieces; cut each slice into strips, 1 inch wide and 2½ inches long. Quarter the zucchini lengthwise; cut each quarter into 2-inch lengths. Place the eggplant and zucchini in a medium-sized bowl; sprinkle with salt, toss, and allow to stand for 30 minutes. Drain the liquid, rinse and dry the vegetables; toss lightly in flour.

In a large skillet, heat 2 tablespoons of the oil over medium-high heat until hot but not smoking; add half of the eggplant-zucchini and sauté until golden. Remove from the pan. Add 2 more tablespoons of the oil and sauté remaining half of eggplant-zucchini; remove from pan. Pour 2 more tablespoons of oil into the skillet, if necessary; add the tofu and sauté for 5 minutes. Mix in the onions, green pepper and garlic; sauté for

3 to 4 minutes. Add the tomatoes, salt and pepper and cook for 5 minutes more.

Combine the cheese and spices in a small bowl. Place ⅓ of the tofu-tomato mixture in a medium-sized skillet, sprinkle with ⅓ of the cheese and spice mixture and top with half of the eggplant-zucchini. Alternate layers of tofu, cheese and eggplant-zucchini, finishing with a layer of cheese on top. Cover and simmer over low heat for 10 minutes. Uncover and simmer for 30 to 45 minutes, or until most of the liquid has been absorbed.

Tofu Nut Loaf

Serves 4

1 cup raw mixed nuts
1 cup fresh whole wheat bread crumbs
1 cup cooked brown rice
1 pound tofu, frozen, thawed and crumbled
1 onion, finely chopped
½ teaspoon sage
½ teaspoon thyme
1 to 1½ teaspoons sea salt
Dash of black pepper
3 tablespoons melted butter
3 dashes Maggi seasoning (available in the
      gourmet section of most supermarkets)
Water to moisten if necessary

Preheat oven to 375° F. Place the nuts in a blender and mix at high speed until finely chopped. Combine all the ingredients except 1 tablespoon of the butter in a bowl, mixing well and adding water to moisten if necessary. Press the mixture into a buttered loaf pan or an 8-inch square baking pan. Bake for 35 minutes, basting with the remaining butter after the first 15 minutes. Serve with gravy or sauce.

Lemon Tofu-Balls

Serves 4 to 6

Sauce:

3 tablespoons butter or cold-pressed olive or soy oil

2 stalks celery, finely chopped

2 large onions, finely chopped

2 carrots, finely chopped

2 teaspoons whole wheat or unbleached white flour

1⅓ cups hot bean stock

Sea salt and freshly ground black pepper to taste

Tofu-Balls:

19 ounces regular tofu, drained for 30 minutes and squeezed

1 teaspoon sea salt

2 large cloves garlic, minced

1 tablespoon freshly grated lemon peel

1 tablespoon fresh parsley, snipped

½ teaspoon ground nutmeg

½ teaspoon thyme

1 egg, slightly beaten

½ cup dry whole wheat bread crumbs, finely ground

1 tablespoon butter

2 tablespoons cold-pressed olive oil

⅓ cup fresh lemon juice

¼ cup Parmesan cheese, freshly grated if possible

Sauce: In a large skillet, melt the butter over medium heat; add the celery, onions and carrots and sauté, uncovered, for 10 minutes or until onion is transparent. Add the flour and stir constantly for 2 minutes until slightly thickened; stir in the stock and simmer for 2 minutes more. Season to taste with salt and pepper and set aside.

Tofu-Balls: In a medium-sized mixing bowl, knead the squeezed tofu as you would bread for 4 minutes; add the salt and garlic and continue kneading for 3 minutes until the tofu is smooth and doughy. Add the lemon peel, parsley, nutmeg and thyme and knead for 2 minutes more. Blend in the beaten egg, stirring with your hands. Roll rounded tea-spoonfuls of the mixture between wetted palms to form "meatballs"; roll in the bread crumbs. In a 10-inch skillet, heat the butter and oil over medium heat; fry the tofu-balls, turning frequently until brown on all sides.

Add the balls to the sauce and simmer, uncovered, for 1 hour. Sprinkle with the lemon juice and cheese. Serve immediately.

Zucchini Descanso

This is a dish my sister made up when our summer garden's crop of zuc-chini had a population explosion.

Serves 4 to 6
¼ cup cold-pressed olive oil
2 large zucchini, thinly sliced, unpeeled
1 onion, chopped
2 whole green onions, chopped
1 green bell pepper, seeded and chopped
¼ pound mushrooms, sliced
1¼ pounds firm tofu, drained for 20 minutes,
    patted dry and cut into ½-inch cubes
2 cloves garlic, minced
2 teaspoons oregano
Sea salt and pepper to taste
1 quart canned tomatoes
8 ounces mozzarella cheese
Sprinkle of crushed red chili peppers (optional)

In a large heavy kettle or soup pot, heat the oil over medium heat; add all of the ingredients except the tomatoes and cheese and sauté, stirring fre-quently, until the onions and zucchini are transparent. Add the tomatoes and half of their liquid to the vegetables. Remove the pot from the heat, cover, and refrigerate for 3 to 4 hours or overnight.

Preheat oven to 275° F. Transfer the zucchini-tomato mixture to a 9″ × 11″ baking dish; sprinkle grated mozzarella on top and bake for 35 minutes or until heated through. Sprinkle with crushed red chili peppers if desired. Serve with steamed brown rice and garden salad.

Tofu and Mushroom Crêpes

Makes approximately 15 crêpes

Crêpes:

2 cups whole wheat pastry flour

½ teaspoon sea salt

4 eggs

2 cups rich soymilk or dairy milk

Filling:

3 tablespoons Willow Run or other soy
    margarine

3 tablespoons whole wheat or unbleached
    white flour

1¼ cups rich soymilk or dairy milk, heated
    almost to a boil

½ teaspoon sea salt

2 tablespoons onion, finely chopped

1 pound mushrooms, sliced

½ pound regular tofu, crumbled

3 tablespoons dry white wine

Approximately 5 tablespoons butter or
    margarine

Crêpes: In a medium-sized bowl, combine the flour and salt; stir in the eggs one at a time. Add milk a little at a time, stirring well after each addition and continue stirring until batter is smooth. Refrigerate for at least 2 hours.

Filling: In a large skillet, melt the margarine over medium heat until foamy, whisk in the flour and cook, stirring continuously, for 3 to 5 minutes or until the mixture is fragrant but not brown. Slowly pour in the warmed milk, whisking continuously to prevent lumps. Add the salt, onion, mushrooms, tofu, and wine; reduce heat and simmer for 20 minutes. Adjust seasoning; place over low heat until crêpes are ready to be filled.

Heat a 7- or 8-inch cast iron pan or a French crêpe pan over medium heat; add approximately 1 teaspoon of butter or margarine to coat the bottom of the pan. When the butter starts to foam, stir the crêpe batter and ladle about ¼ cup into the pan. Tip the pan to coat the bottom evenly with the batter; cook until the crêpe is firm enough to turn over. Flip with a spatula and cook for 1 to 2 minutes, or until both sides are lightly browned. Cook remaining batter, lightly buttering the pan between crêpes. Keep crêpes in a warm oven or wrapped in a towel until ready to fill.

Spoon 2 to 3 tablespoons of tofu-mushroom mixture in the center of each crêpe; roll the sides up around the filling.

VARIATION: For breakfast or dessert, use the Tofu-Strawberry Delight found in the dessert section as filling and top with whipped cream.

Stuffed Green Peppers

Serves 4

4 large green bell peppers
1 cup boiling water
1 teaspoon sea salt
1½ pounds firm or regular tofu, frozen, thawed
    and crumbled
¼ cup onion, minced
¼ cup celery, minced
1 teaspoon sea salt
1 egg
½ cup evaporated milk
1 cup cooked brown rice

Sauce:
1 quart canned tomatoes
¼ cup onion, minced
½ teaspoon sea salt
1 tablespoon raw sugar
¼ teaspoon cinnamon
½ teaspoon ground cloves
1 tablespoon whole wheat or unbleached white
    flour
¼ cup cold water

Cut out the core of each pepper without slicing the outer shell. Rinse the peppers and place in the boiling water with the salt. Cover and cook for 5 minutes; remove from the water and drain upside down on paper towels or newspaper. In a medium-sized bowl, combine the tofu, onions, celery, salt, egg, milk, and rice; adjust seasoning to taste. Stuff the peppers with the tofu mixture. Place in a square baking dish.

Sauce: Preheat oven to 350° F. In a small saucepan, combine the tomatoes, onion, salt, sugar, cinnamon, and cloves; simmer, uncovered, over low heat for 10 minutes. Stir the flour into the cold water until smooth and add to the sauce. Cook over medium heat until slightly thickened. Pour the sauce over the peppers. Bake for 45 to 50 minutes.

VARIATION: Use the filling to stuff chard or cabbage leaves. Lightly steam the chard or cabbage; put one or two tablespoonfuls of filling inside the leaves and roll up, fastening with toothpicks if necessary. Place the seam side down in a baking dish; cover with sauce, and bake as directed.

Crustless Quiche

My mom came up with this recipe one summer when my sisters and I all wanted quiche, but didn't want the crust.

> Serves 4 to 6
> 2 medium-sized or 4 to 5 small summer or
>   zucchini squash, unpeeled and thinly sliced
> ¾ cup each Cheddar, Monterey Jack and Swiss
>   Cheese, grated
> ⅓ cup Ortega-brand chilies, diced
> ½ pound regular tofu, crumbled
> 2 long dashes A-1 or Maggi Seasoning
>   (all-natural products)
> ½ teaspoon basil
> ½ teaspoon oregano
> ¼ teaspoon marjoram
> Sea salt and pepper to taste
> 2 eggs
> ⅓ cup milk

Preheat oven to 350° F. Place the squash in a steamer or in a saucepan with 3 to 4 tablespoons water and steam over medium heat until tender, but crunchy. Line the bottom and sides of a 9-inch pie plate with the squash slices. Sprinkle with cheddar cheese, chilies, tofu, Jack cheese, spices and Swiss cheese, in that order.

In a small bowl, whisk the eggs until light and frothy; add the milk and pour over the top of the quiche. Bake for 45 minutes to 1 hour. Cool for 10 minutes. Slice and serve with a hearty green salad and sliced tomatoes.

Tofu Stroganoff

Serves 4 to 6
1 tablespoon butter
3 tablespoons cold-pressed soy oil
2 pounds firm tofu, drained, pressed and cut
    into slices ½ inch thick and 2 inches long
Dash of shoyu (natural soy sauce)
½ cup whole green onions, thinly sliced
½ pound mushrooms, thinly sliced
1 tablespoon whole wheat or unbleached white
    flour
½ cup white wine
½ cup sour cream
1 tablespoon heavy tomato purée
1 teaspoon sea salt or to taste
Freshly ground black pepper to taste
2 tablespoons fresh parsley, finely chopped

In a heavy 12-inch skillet, heat the butter and 2 tablespoons of the oil over medium heat until butter foams; add the tofu. Sprinkle with shoyu and fry the tofu until lightly browned on both sides. With a slotted spoon, transfer to a plate.

Pour the remaining oil into the skillet; add the onions and mushrooms and sauté, stirring often, for 3 to 4 minutes, or until lightly browned. Gradually mix in the flour, wine and sour cream, stirring constantly. Blend in the tomato purée, salt and pepper. Add the fried tofu, coating thoroughly with the sauce. Cover and simmer for 2 to 3 minutes, or until heated through. Adjust seasoning to taste. Transfer to a serving platter. Sprinkle with parsley and serve with noodles or brown rice.

Tofu Chow Mein

Serves 4

3 tablespoons peanut or sesame oil
2 pounds firm tofu, drained for 20 minutes, pressed for 15 minutes and cut into ¼-inch strips
4 tablespoons shoyu (natural soy sauce)
2 cloves garlic, finely chopped
1 medium onion, cut in half lengthwise, then crosswise into ¼-inch crescents
2 stalks celery, cut into 4-inch lengths, ⅛ inch wide
1 cup bok choy or white cabbage, finely shredded
1 cup snow peas, fresh if possible
½ cup canned water chestnuts, drained and thinly sliced
½ pound fresh mushrooms, sliced
1½ cups bean sprouts
1½ teaspoons sea salt
1¾ cups water or bean stock
2 tablespoons arrowroot or corn starch
½ cup toasted almonds, slivered or chopped

In a wok or heavy 10-inch skillet, heat the oil until very hot but not smoking; add the tofu and braise over medium-high heat for 4 minutes. Sprinkle with 1 tablespoon shoyu. Add the garlic and vegetables and sauté for 2 to 3 minutes, stirring constantly. Sprinkle with salt, pour in the remaining shoyu and 1¼ cups of the water or stock. Cover the pan and cook over medium heat for 6 to 8 minutes, until vegetables are tender but still firm.

Dissolve the arrowroot in the remaining water; stir into the chow mein. Cook for 30 seconds until the sauce is clear and thick. Remove pan from heat; transfer contents to a platter and sprinkle with almonds. Serve at once with steamed brown rice.

Tofu-Vegetable Burritos

Serves 4 to 6

2 tablespoons cold-pressed soy oil
1 large onion, thinly sliced
2 cloves garlic, minced
1 pound tofu, frozen, defrosted and crumbled
½ pound mushrooms, sliced
1 large bell pepper, diced
2 medium carrots, diced
4 medium zucchini, sliced
2 large tomatoes, chopped
¾ cup Ortega-brand green chilies, diced
1 teaspoon chili powder
1 teaspoon sea salt
½ teaspoon cuminos
½ teaspoon oregano
1 cup Jack cheese, grated
10 to 12 whole wheat flour tortillas
Guacamole Dip to garnish
Sour cream to garnish
Hot sauce to garnish

In a large skillet, heat the oil over medium heat; add the onion, garlic and tofu and sauté until onion is limp. Add the mushrooms, pepper, carrot, zucchini, tomatoes, chilies, and spices; bring to a boil, reduce heat, cover, and simmer for 10 minutes or until vegetables are barely tender. Stir in half of the cheese; spoon the mixture into a shallow casserole dish and sprinkle with remaining cheese. Place under a broiler and broil until the cheese is melted and bubbly.

Preheat oven to 350° F. Wrap the tortillas in foil and bake until hot, about 20 minutes. To serve, place a tablespoonful of vegetable mixture in the center of each tortilla; top with Guacamole, sour cream and hot sauce and fold up the ends and sides of the tortilla to cover the filling.

Tofu Creole

Usually made with shrimp, this dish adapts itself well to tofu.

> Serves 8
> ⅓ cup + 2 tablespoons cold-pressed soy oil
> 3 pounds regular tofu, drained for 1 hour and
>   cut into 1-inch cubes
> Dash of shoyu (natural soy sauce)
> 2 cups onions, coarsely chopped
> 1 cup green pepper, coarsely chopped
> 1 cup celery, coarsely chopped
> 2 teaspoons garlic, finely chopped
> 4 cups canned tomatoes, drained and coarsely
>   chopped
> 1 cup water
> 2 medium bay leaves
> 2 to 3 teaspoons paprika or to taste
> ¼ to ½ teaspoon cayenne (red) pepper or to
>   taste
> 1 tablespoon sea salt
> 2 tablespoons arrowroot or cornstarch,
>   dissolved in ¼ cup cold water
> 6 to 8 cups freshly cooked brown rice

In a 4- or 5-quart casserole, heat 2 tablespoons of the oil over high heat; when the oil is very hot add the tofu and braise, stirring frequently with a spatula to prevent sticking. Sprinkle the tofu with shoyu (it will smoke and splatter); cook for 3 to 4 minutes more or until firm and browned. Remove from pan and set aside.

Pour the remaining oil into the casserole and heat over medium heat until lightly hazy. Add the onions, green peppers, celery and garlic and sauté for 5 minutes, or until vegetables are soft and translucent but not brown, stirring frequently. Add the tomatoes, braised tofu, water, bay leaves, paprika, cayenne and salt; stir and bring to a boil over high heat. Reduce heat, cover partially, and simmer for 30 minutes, stirring occasionally. Stir in the dissolved arrowroot; simmer for 2 to 3 minutes, or until the sauce thickens slightly, stirring constantly. Discard the bay leaves; adjust seasoning to taste. Serve with rice.

Tofu Chops

These are traditionally made with crab, but this version of ganmo is very tasty.

Serves 4 to 6

3 cups regular tofu, drained and squeezed
2 cloves garlic, minced
¼ cup parsley, finely chopped
¼ cup whole green onions, finely chopped
3 teaspoons sea salt
10 tablespoons butter
¼ cup flour, whole wheat pastry or unbleached
    white
1 cup milk
½ teaspoon cayenne (red) pepper
3 eggs
3 cups fresh whole wheat bread crumbs
Cold-pressed soy or corn oil for deep-frying
1 lemon, sliced for garnish
Homemade thousand island dressing

In a medium-sized mixing bowl, knead the drained and squeezed tofu for 5 minutes; add the garlic, parsley, green onions and 2 teaspoons of the salt, and knead for 3 minutes more, or until tofu is smooth and doughy. Set aside.

In a heavy saucepan, melt the butter over medium heat; add the flour, mixing well. Stirring constantly with a wire whisk, pour in the milk in a slow, thin stream; cook over high heat until the mixture comes to a boil, thickens, and becomes smooth. Reduce heat and simmer, uncovered, for 2 to 3 minutes. Stir in the cayenne pepper and the remaining teaspoon of salt. Remove the pan from heat; add the flour mixture to the tofu mixture and blend well. Adjust seasoning to taste. Cover the bowl with a towel and refrigerate for at least 2 hours.

In a shallow bowl, beat the eggs to a froth with a wire whisk. Spread the bread crumbs on a platter. Divide the tofu mixture into 8 to 12 equal portions and shape each portion into a tear-drop-shaped "chop" about ½ inch thick. Place each chop in the bread crumbs and coat both sides; dip into the egg and into the crumbs again to bread it evenly. Place the chops side-by-side on a large pan and refrigerate for ½ hour.

In a wok or heavy pot, heat approximately 3 inches of oil to 375° F. on a deep-fry or candy thermometer. Fry the chops, 1 or 2 at a time, for 3 to 4 minutes, or until the coating is crisp and browned. Drain on paper towels or newspaper. Garnish with lemon and serve with thousand island dressing for dipping. Accompany with a steamed grain and steamed broccoli or asparagus.

Broiled Tofu Steaks
with Garlic and Herb Butter

Serves 4

Garlic butter:
4 tablespoons soft butter
1 tablespoon green onions, finely chopped
1 clove garlic, minced
2 tablespoons fresh parsley, finely chopped
Sea salt and pepper to taste

Tofu Steaks:
19 ounces firm tofu, drained for 10 minutes,
    sliced into 1½-inch-thick pieces and
    pressed for 20 minutes
2 tablespoons melted butter
Sea salt and freshly ground black pepper
2 lemons, cut into slices

Butter: Using a wooden spoon, cream the butter in a small bowl until fluffy; beat in the spices. Set aside.

Tofu: Preheat the broiler for 15 minutes. Dry the tofu with a towel; using a pastry brush, spread the melted butter on both sides of each tofu steak. Broil 3 to 4 inches from the broiler for 3 minutes on each side. Sprinkle with salt and pepper to taste; spread with garlic butter. Serve garnished with lemon slices.

Tofu with Mushrooms
in White Wine Sauce

Serves 6

Tofu:

2 tablespoons cold-pressed soy oil

2 pounds firm tofu, drained for 30 minutes and
    cut into 1-inch cubes

Few sprinklings of shoyu (natural soy sauce)

1½ cups water

1½ cups white wine

3 green onions, sliced

3 celery tops with leaves, cut into 2-inch pieces

4 parsley sprigs

1 bay leaf

10 peppercorns

¾ pound mushrooms, sliced

Sauce:

4 tablespoons butter

5 tablespoons whole wheat or unbleached
    white flour

1 cup rich soymilk or ¾ cup dairy milk and
    ¼ cup cream

2 egg yolks

3 drops fresh lemon juice, strained

1½ to 2 teaspoons sea salt

Freshly ground black pepper

2 cloves garlic, minced

½ teaspoon marjoram

¼ teaspoon basil

¼ cup Swiss cheese, grated

Tofu: In a heavy skillet, heat the oil over medium heat until lightly hazy; add the tofu and sauté for 10 minutes. Transfer to a bowl, sprinkle with shoyu, and allow to stand. In a heavy 3-quart pot, combine the water, wine, onions, celery, parsley, bay leaf, and peppercorns and bring to a boil over high heat; reduce heat and simmer, uncovered, for 20 minutes. Strain the stock through a sieve into the heavy skillet, discarding the vegetables. Add the tofu and mushrooms, cover, and simmer for 8 minutes. With a slotted spoon, remove the tofu and mushrooms to a large bowl. Boil down remaining stock to 1 cup.

Sauce: In a 3-quart pot, melt the butter over medium heat. Lift the pan from heat and stir in the flour. Return to low heat and cook, stirring constantly, for 1 to 2 minutes, but do not brown. Remove the pan from heat and slowly add the stock and the milk, whisking constantly. Return the pan to high heat and cook, stirring constantly with a whisk until thick and boiling; reduce heat and simmer for 1 minute.

In a small bowl, beat the egg yolks; gradually stir in 4 tablespoons of the sauce. Whisk the egg mixture into the pot of sauce. Over medium heat, boil for 30 seconds, stirring constantly. Remove from heat and add lemon juice and spices. The sauce should be thick enough to coat a spoon; if too thick, thin with more soymilk.

Preheat oven to 350° F. With a baster, draw up any juice in the tofu and mushrooms (save for preparing soup). Pour the sauce over the tofu and stir gently. Butter six shallow custard cups; spoon in the mixture and sprinkle with grated cheese. Bake for 10 to 15 minutes or until the sauce bubbles, then slide under a hot broiler for 3 seconds to brown the top. Serve immediately.

Tofu Curry

Serves 4 to 6

⅓ cup + 1 tablespoon cold-pressed soy oil

2 pounds firm tofu, drained for 20 minutes,
  pressed for 15 minutes, and cut into 1-inch
  cubes

Sprinkle of shoyu (natural soy sauce)

2 teaspoons fresh ginger root, scraped and
  finely chopped

½ teaspoon garlic, finely chopped

1½ teaspoons sea salt

3 medium onions, cut into ⅛-inch slices

2 tablespoons curry powder (such as Madras-
  brand)

1 teaspoon ground coriander

1 teaspoon ground anise seed

½ teaspoon cinnamon

3 medium-sized tomatoes, firm and ripe, cut
  into ¼-inch slices

3 tablespoons fresh lemon juice, strained

½ cup water

In a heavy 12-inch skillet, heat the oil over high heat until very hot but not smoking; add the tofu and braise, stirring continuously to prevent sticking. Sprinkle with shoyu and stir for 3 to 4 minutes more, or until the tofu is firm and browned. Transfer to a bowl and set aside.

With a mortar and pestle, crush the ginger, garlic and salt to a dry paste; set aside.

In the heavy skillet, heat the remaining oil over medium heat until a light haze forms; add the onions and cook until soft and golden brown, stirring frequently. Add the curry powder, coriander, anise seed and cinnamon and stir for 2 minutes; stir in the ginger and garlic paste, tomatoes, braised tofu, lemon juice and water and bring to a boil. Reduce heat and simmer, stirring frequently, until the tomatoes are tender and begin to break apart. Cover tightly and simmer for 15 minutes; adjust seasoning to taste. Serve with rice, sliced cucumbers, yoghurt and condiments such as raisins, peanuts, and coconut.

Tofu Loaf Sandwich

This is a popular sandwich in New Orleans, made with oysters instead of tofu.

Serves 4

3 cups regular tofu, drained and squeezed

2 cloves garlic, minced

¼ cup whole green onions, finely chopped

2⅛ teaspoons sea salt

2 eggs

½ cup evaporated milk

1 cup corn or whole wheat pastry flour

1½ cups fresh whole wheat bread crumbs

1 15-inch loaf French or Italian bread

Homemade or Hain-brand Italian dressing

Cold-pressed soy oil for deep-frying

Homemade or honey-sweetened mayonnaise

1½ cups finely shredded lettuce or sprouts

1 large tomato, sliced

In a medium-sized bowl, knead the tofu for 5 minutes; add the garlic, green onions, and 2 teaspoons of the salt, and knead for 3 minutes more, or until tofu is smooth and doughy. Set aside.

In a shallow bowl, beat the eggs with a wire whisk; add the milk and the remaining ⅛ teaspoon salt, mixing well. Spread the flour and the bread crumbs on separate sheets of waxed paper. Shape the tofu into patties about 2½ inches across and ½ inch thick. Roll each patty in the flour until evenly coated; dip into the egg mixture and roll again in the crumbs. Refrigerate for 30 minutes to set.

Preheat oven to 350° F. Slice the bread in half lengthwise; scrape out the inner dough to form two shells. With a pastry brush, brush both sides of the bread shells with Italian dressing; place on a baking sheet and bake for 15 minutes or until crisp and light brown.

In a wok or heavy saucepan, heat 3 inches of oil to 375° F. on a deep-fry or candy thermometer. Fry the tofu patties, turning with a slotted spoon every 2 to 3 minutes until the coating is crisp and golden brown; drain on paper towels or newspaper.

Spread the mayonnaise on the bread halves; arrange lettuce or sprouts on the bottom half, tomato slices and tofu on the top and close the sandwich. Slice in quarters and serve.

Lasagne

Like the Enchiladas, this is one of my favorite dishes—one I serve often to company. The sauce recipe has been in my family for as long as I can remember. It was a "Sunday" dish—a special treat. It is especially good when combined with the creamy taste of tofu.

Serves 8

Sauce:

3 tablespoons cold-pressed olive oil
1½ cups onion, chopped
2 cloves garlic, minced
4 6-ounce cans tomato paste or heavy tomato
    purée
7 cups canned tomatoes
2 cups water or 1¼ cup water plus ¾ cup red
    wine
½ tablespoon honey
1 tablespoon sea salt
½ teaspoon ground pepper
1 tablespoon oregano, crushed, or 1½ tea-
    spoons oregano plus 1½ teaspoons Italian
    Herb Seasoning
2 bay leaves
1 carrot, grated

Filling:

1½ to 1¾ pounds tofu, drained for 20 minutes
    and patted dry
8 ounces sour cream
1 bunch whole green onions, finely chopped
1½ teaspoons sea salt
Dash of black pepper
1 to 2 teaspoons honey or to taste
¼ teaspoon paprika

4 quarts water
1 tablespoon cold-pressed soy oil
8 ounces lasagne noodles (whole wheat or soy
    or spinach)
Sliced mushrooms and black olives to garnish
    (optional)

Sauce: In a large kettle, heat the oil over medium heat; add the onion and garlic and sauté until tender but not brown. Add the remaining sauce ingredients, stirring well; reduce heat and simmer, uncovered, for 30 minutes. Remove the bay leaves and cook for 30 minutes more. The longer the sauce simmers, the thicker it gets; thin with water as needed.

Filling: In a medium-sized bowl, break up the tofu. Add the sour cream and blend until very smooth. Add the onions, salt, pepper, honey and paprika. Adjust seasoning to taste and set aside.

In a large kettle, boil the water and oil. Add the noodles and cook for 15 minutes, or until tender but not mushy; drain in a large colander.

Preheat oven to 325° F. Cover the bottom of a 13″ × 15″ pan with sauce. Alternate layers of noodles, tofu filling and sauce, finishing with a layer of tofu on top. Garnish with sliced mushrooms and black olives if desired. Bake for 30 minutes or until heated through; turn off heat and allow lasagne to stand for 15 to 20 minutes with the oven door cracked. Serve with spinach salad and hot garlic bread.

VARIATIONS: Add layers of slightly steamed fresh spinach with the tofu and sauce.

Replace the noodles with lengthwise strips of fresh zucchini, about ¼-inch-thick for a rich meal low in calories.

Use the sauce and filling to make manicotti or large baked shell noodles.

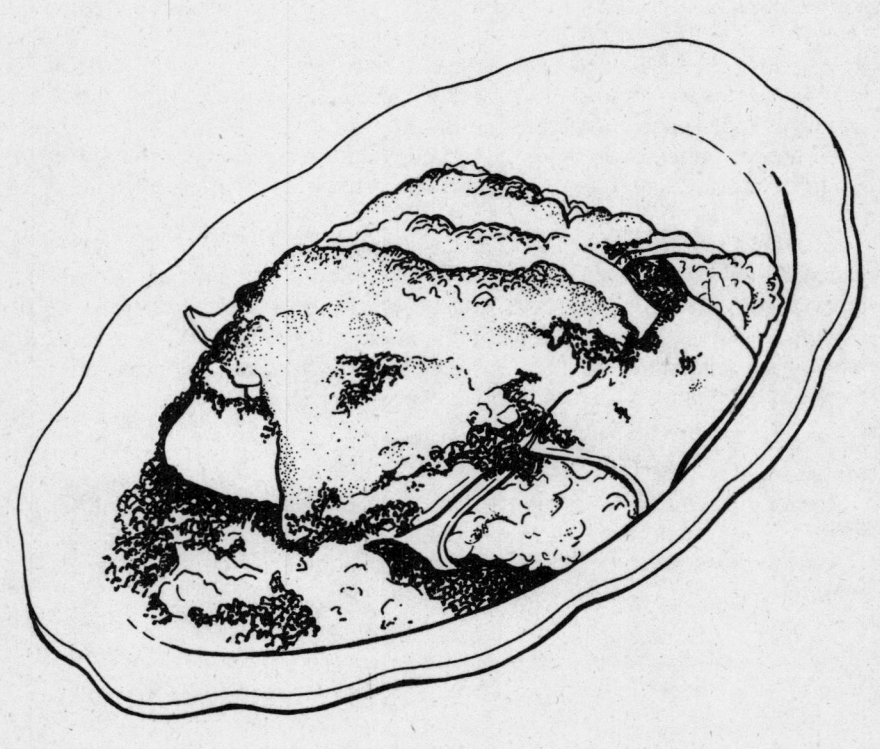

Sweet and Sour Tofu

Serves 2

2 eggs, lightly beaten

¼ cup whole wheat or unbleached white flour

2 tablespoons arrowroot or cornstarch

2 tablespoons dry sherry

½ teaspoon sea salt

1½ pounds firm tofu, drained for 20 minutes, pressed for 20 minutes and cut into ¾-inch cubes

Sauce:

4 to 6 tablespoons honey

6 tablespoons cider or wine vinegar

2 teaspoons shoyu (natural soy sauce)

¼ cup tomato purée or tomato paste

1 teaspoon arrowroot or cornstarch

½ teaspoon Tabasco sauce (this is an all-natural sauce)

¼ cup bean broth or water

Cold-pressed soy oil for deep-frying

1 medium-sized carrot, diced

6 dried black mushrooms (available in the gourmet section of supermarkets or in Oriental grocers), soaked for ½ hour in hot water and patted dry

1 cup broccoli flower tops, sliced

2 teaspoons fresh ginger, minced

In a small bowl, combine the eggs, flour, arrowroot, sherry and salt; add the tofu and coat thoroughly. Refrigerate for 30 minutes.

In a small bowl, combine all the sauce ingredients. Set aside. In a wok, heat about 3 inches oil over high heat to 350° F. on a deep-fry or candy thermometer; add the tofu and fry until golden brown. Remove tofu with a slotted spoon and drain on paper towels or newspaper.

Pour off all but 2 tablespoons of the oil; add the carrots, mushrooms and broccoli and stir-fry for 1 minute. Add the ginger and stir-fry for 5 seconds. Add the tofu to wok; mix in the sauce and stir-fry over medium-high heat until hot and well mixed. Serve immediately.

Quickie Tofu Sandwich

Makes 2 open-faced sandwiches
2 to 3 tablespoons cold-pressed soy oil
1 pound firm tofu, drained for 10 minutes,
    sliced into 4 pieces and pressed for
    30 minutes
Sprinkle of shoyu (natural soy sauce)
Sprinkle of pepper
2 slices whole wheat bread
Mustard to garnish
Mayonnaise to garnish
½ medium onion, cut into thin crescents
5 medium-sized mushrooms, sliced
½ cup sprouts
½ medium tomato, sliced
Sprinkle of grated cheese

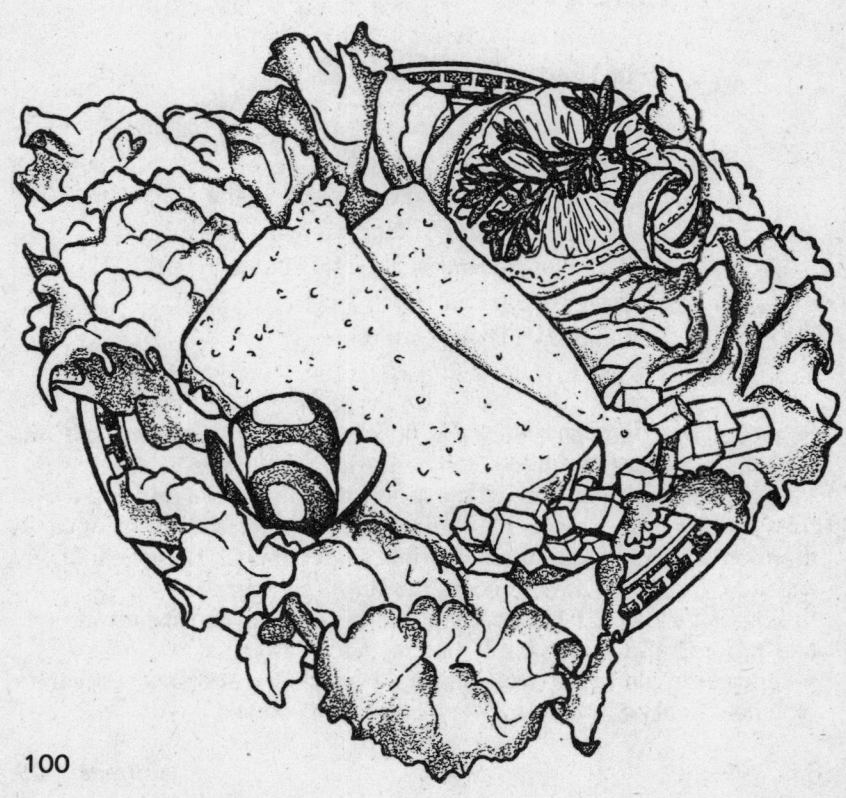

In a large skillet, heat the oil over medium heat until lightly hazy. Add the tofu slices and sauté until browned on both sides. Sprinkle each slice with shoyu and pepper; remove and drain on newspaper or paper towels.

Spread a slice of whole wheat bread with mustard and mayonnaise; cover with a layer of tofu. Garnish with sliced onions and mushrooms, sprouts, and tomatoes; sprinkle grated cheese on top and place under a broiler until cheese is melted and bubbly. Serve immediately with tortilla chips and potato salad.

Quick Sautéed Tofu and Mushrooms

Serves 2 to 3
2 to 3 tablespoons cold-pressed soy oil
1 pound firm tofu, drained for 10 minutes,
    pressed for 20 to 30 minutes and cut into
    1-inch pieces
10 medium-sized mushrooms, sliced
½ large onion, cut into thin crescents
Sprinkle of shoyu (natural soy sauce)
Pepper
½ to ¾ cup Jack cheese, grated

In a large skillet, heat the oil over medium-high heat until lightly hazy. Add the tofu and sauté, turning frequently, until browned on all sides. Mix in the mushrooms and onions, and sauté for 5 minutes. Reduce heat, sprinkle generously with shoyu, and sauté, turning continuously, for 5 minutes more. Remove the pan from heat; top with grated cheese, sprinkle with pepper and place under a broiler for several minutes, or until cheese is completely melted. Serve with whole wheat toast and sliced tomatoes.

VARIATION: Spoon the tofu mixture into hot corn tortillas; fold like a taco, and garnish with sprouts, avocado, and homemade hot sauce.

Desserts

Rosielie's Chocolate Mousse Cheese Cake

Serves 8

3 pounds regular tofu, drained for 20 minutes
    and patted dry
1 egg
½ teaspoon sea salt
1 pint sour cream
½ teaspoon vanilla
4 tablespoons whole wheat pastry or
    unbleached white flour
1 cup honey
2 tablespoons hot water
2 tablespoons Pero (instant cereal beverage) or
    instant coffee
2 tablespoons butter
3 squares unsweetened baking chocolate
½ cup granola, ground in the blender until fine
    crumbs

In a blender or large mixing bowl, combine the tofu, egg, salt, sour cream, vanilla, flour and honey, and mix at medium speed for 2 to 3 minutes until smooth, stopping when necessary to scrape down sides with a spatula. Dissolve the Pero or coffee in the hot water, add to the tofu mixture and blend again.

In the top of a double boiler, melt the butter and chocolate; add to the tofu mixture and blend well.

Preheat oven to 350° F. Butter the bottom and sides of a 9-inch spring-form pan and dust with granola crumbs. Pour the tofu mixture into the pan; bake for 1 hour. Cool on a wire rack. Refrigerate for at least 8 hours before serving.

Apple Torte

Serves 8 to 10

Pastry:

1½ cups whole wheat pastry flour
1 cup ground almonds
⅓ cup honey-flakes (found in natural food
    stores)
¼ teaspoon sea salt
¼ teaspoon cinnamon
½ cup Willow Run soy margarine or regular
    margarine
1 egg

Filling:

3 pounds pippin or Granny Smith apples,
    unpeeled and sliced into ¼-inch slices
1 tablespoon lemon juice
4 tablespoons butter
1 pound regular tofu, squeezed and crumbled
5 tablespoons honey
¼ cup whole wheat pastry or unbleached white
    flour
¼ teaspoon nutmeg
Dash of cinnamon
Dash of coriander

¼ cup honey-sweetened orange marmalade
¼ cup honey-sweetened red raspberry
    preserves

Pastry: In a small bowl, combine the dry pastry ingredients; cut in the margarine until the mixture resembles coarse crumbs. Stir in the egg until the
dough no longer sticks to the sides of the bowl. Remove ⅓ cup
of the dough and set aside. Press remaining dough into a 9-inch springform pan to form a crust across the bottom and 1½ inches up the sides.
Refrigerate.

Filling: In a large bowl, toss the apple slices lightly with the lemon juice. In a large skillet, heat 2 tablespoons of the butter over medium heat; add half of the apple slices and cook, stirring gently, until the edges of the apples soften. With a slotted spoon, transfer to a large bowl; add the remaining butter, cook the other half of the apples and remove. Add the crumbled tofu to the butter remaining in the pan and sauté until light, fluffy, and fragrant. Mix the tofu with the sliced apples; sprinkle with flour, nutmeg, cinnamon, and coriander, and stir lightly to coat evenly.

Preheat oven to 425° F. Spoon the tofu-apple mixture into the chilled pastry. On a well-floured surface, roll the reserved pastry dough into a 9" × 3" rectangle. Cut into 4 strips and place across the top of the apples to form two X's; press at the sides to seal. Bake for 10 minutes. Lower heat to 350° F. and bake for 20 minutes longer. Brush the top of the torte with orange marmalade and bake for 10 to 15 minutes longer. Remove the torte from the oven and cool on a wire rack for 15 minutes; spoon melted raspberry preserves over the filling. Serve warm or cold, with whipped cream if desired.

Tofu-Rice Pudding

Serves 4

2 cups cooked brown rice
½ pound regular tofu, crumbled
⅓ cup pure maple syrup or honey
½ cup raisins, simmered in orange juice to
     cover for 15 minutes, and drained
2 small apples, unpeeled and thinly sliced
1 teaspoon butter

Preheat oven to 350° F. Combine the rice, tofu, and syrup or honey in a mixing bowl; add the raisins and apples, stirring well. Spoon the mixture into a small casserole dish; top with the butter, cover, and bake for 40 minutes. Serve with cream or milk if desired.

Tofu Black Bottom Pie

Serves 6 to 8

Pastry:

¼ cup butter

1 tablespoon honey

2 cups granola or graham crackers, whirled in
    the blender to crumb consistency

Filling:

6 heaping tablespoons agar flakes

¾ cup boiling water

2 pounds regular tofu, drained for 20 minutes
    and patted dry

1 cup honey

4 ounces unsweetened baking chocolate,
    melted

¼ cup butter, melted

2 teaspoons vanilla

2 teaspoons cinnamon

Pastry: Preheat oven to 300° F. In a small pan, melt the butter; add the honey, stirring to dissolve. Pour the honey into a mixing bowl with the granola or graham cracker crumbs and mix well. Press the mixture into a 9- or 10-inch pie pan to form a crust. Bake for 5 minutes.

Filling: In a saucepan, dissolve the agar flakes in boiling water; reduce heat and stir well for 2 minutes until very thick. If mixture thickens too quickly, remove from heat and continue to stir for the full 2 minutes. In a blender, combine 1 pound of the tofu, ½ cup of the honey and half of the dissolved agar; blend at medium speed for 2 to 3 minutes, or until creamy, stopping when necessary to scrape down the sides with a spatula. Add the melted chocolate and blend again. Carefully spread the blended mixture over the pie crust.

Wash the blender thoroughly; combine the remaining 1 pound of tofu, ½ cup honey, and remaining agar in it. Blend well at medium speed for 2 to 3 minutes, stopping and scraping when necessary. Add the melted butter, vanilla and cinnamon, and blend for 2 to 3 minutes more. Carefully spread the mixture over the chocolate tofu; refrigerate for at least 6 hours or overnight. Just before serving top decoratively with whipped cream and shaved, semi-sweet chocolate.

Tofu Ice Cream Cake

This is a very rich, very dense cake, so go lightly!

> Serves 8 to 10
> 1 pound regular tofu, drained for 20 minutes
>   and patted dry
> 1 teaspoon vanilla
> 1 tablespoon cinnamon
> ½ teaspoon sea salt
> ¼ cup butter, melted
> 6 tablespoons carob powder
> 1 cup honey
> 2 cups walnut meal (walnuts chopped in a
>   blender until fine)
> 2 cups whole wheat pastry or unbleached white
>   flour
> 2 tablespoons baking powder (Rumford's is the
>   purest)
> ½ pint whipping cream
> 1 cup carob chips
> 1 quart very hard, honey-sweetened vanilla ice
>   cream (rectangular carton)
> Whipped cream to garnish

Preheat oven to 350° F. In a blender, combine the tofu, vanilla, cinnamon and salt; mix at medium speed for 2 to 3 minutes until creamy, stopping when necessary to scrape down the sides with a spatula. In a saucepan, melt the butter, carob powder and honey over medium heat; add to the tofu mixture in the blender and mix well at medium speed for 2 minutes. In a small bowl, mix the walnut meal, flour and baking powder together; combine with the tofu mixture in a mixing bowl. Fold in the whipping cream and stir in the carob chips.

Butter the bottom and sides of a 9-inch springform pan; pour the batter into the pan. Bake for 2 hours. Cool on a wire rack and refrigerate for at least 6 hours before serving. While baking, the cake will settle in the middle, forming a well.

To serve, slice the cake into two layers; cut slabs of vanilla ice cream and place on top of the bottom layer. Replace the top layer and fill the well with whipped cream. Serve immediately.

Lemon-Berry Torte

This is a cool, delicious, elegant and beautiful dessert. The contrasting colors of the lemon and berry make it a visual delight!

Serves 8

Pastry:

1 cup rolled oats
½ cup unsweetened, shredded coconut
1 tablespoon date or raw sugar

Filling:

16 ounces unsweetened, frozen blackberries
    (or other frozen berries)
½ cup berry liquid (from the drained berries)
2 pounds regular tofu, drained for 20 minutes
    and patted dry
1 cup plain or lemon flavored yoghurt
    (unsweetened or honey-sweetened)
½ tablespoon vanilla
1 tablespoon lemon extract
1 tablespoon + 1 teaspoon sesame tahini
    (found in natural food stores or Middle
    Eastern markets)
¼ teaspoon sea salt
7 heaping tablespoons agar flakes
½ cup hot water
1¼ cups honey

Pastry: Butter the sides and bottom of a 9-inch springform pan. In a small bowl, combine all the pastry ingredients and blend well. Press evenly into the bottom and up the sides of the pan to form a crust. Refrigerate.

Filling: Thaw and drain the berries in a colander, over a medium-sized bowl, reserving the liquid. Combine the tofu, yoghurt, vanilla, lemon extract, tahini and salt in a blender, and mix well at medium speed for 2 to 3 minutes, stopping when necessary to scrape down the sides with a spatula.

In a small pan, dissolve 4 tablespoons of the agar in the hot water and stir over low heat for two minutes, or until thick. Remove from heat. In a separate bowl, blend 1 cup of the tofu mixture with the thickened agar; add to the remaining tofu in the blender and mix well at medium speed for 2 to 3 minutes. In a small pan, heat the berry liquid over low heat to almost boiling; add the remaining agar and stir until thickened. Combine the berries and honey in a medium-sized bowl. Slowly add the thickened berry liquid, mixing well.

Preheat oven to 350° F. Remove the crust from the refrigerator and spread with the tofu mixture. Carefully spread the berry mixture on top of the tofu. Bake for 45 minutes. Refrigerate overnight.

Bubby's Hawaiian Fruit Pudding

Serves 8

3 large pippin or Granny Smith apples,
    unpeeled and thinly sliced
½ pound regular tofu, crumbled
½ fresh pineapple, cut into small dice and
    drained, or 1 medium can unsweetened
    pineapple, drained
1½ to 2 cups homemade cranberry sauce
    (made with honey, orange juice and
    cloves)
¾ cup whole wheat pastry flour
⅛ teaspoon sea salt
¼ cup walnuts, coarsely chopped
6 tablespoons Willow Run soy margarine or
    butter
Approximately ½ teaspoon honey

Preheat oven to 350° F. In a lightly buttered 8" × 10" baking dish, place a layer of sliced apples on the bottom; top with layers of tofu, pineapple, and cranberry sauce, in that order.

In a small bowl, combine the flour, salt and walnuts; cut in the margarine until the mixture is in small chunks. Crumble the mixture evenly over the cranberry sauce in the pan. Bake for 30 minutes, or until the apples are tender when pierced with a fork. Drizzle the honey on top and return to the oven. Bake until bubbly and golden on top.

Tofu Pudding in Syrup

Serves 4 to 6

½ to ¾ cup honey
1 teaspoon vanilla
2 cinnamon sticks, broken
1⅓ cups water
½ cup orange juice
2 cloves
1½ pounds regular tofu, drained for 5 minutes,
    pressed for 30 minutes and cut into 1-inch
    squares

In a deep saucepan, combine the honey, vanilla, cinnamon, water, orange juice and cloves. Place over medium heat and boil for 5 to 10 minutes. Remove from heat; adjust seasoning to taste. Carefully add the tofu to the hot syrup. Chill before serving. This pudding will keep covered and refrigerated for up to 2 weeks, although it is best the second or third day.

Tofu Strawberry Delight

Serves 4 to 6

3 pints fresh strawberries, washed, hulled and
    cut in half
2 oranges, peeled, seeded and diced
3 tablespoons honey
1 pound regular tofu, drained for 20 minutes,
    pressed for 30 minutes and cut into ½-inch
    cubes
2 tablespoons orange liqueur
Whipped cream to garnish if desired

In a large bowl, combine all the ingredients except the whipped cream and stir gently. Refrigerate for 1 hour before serving. Serve topped with whipped cream.

Tofu Blintzes

Serves 6

Filling:

1 pound regular tofu, drained for 30 minutes
2 tablespoons + 1 teaspoon honey
1 teaspoon vanilla
1 teaspoon tahini (found in Middle Eastern or
    natural food stores)
1 tablespoon fresh lemon juice, strained
¼ teaspoon sea salt

Blintz:

¾ cup whole wheat pastry or unbleached white
    flour
1 cup half and half
½ teaspoon cinnamon
½ teaspoon sea salt
2 tablespoons cold-pressed soy or corn oil
2 eggs

1 to 2 tablespoons butter for frying

In a blender, combine all the filling ingredients and mix well at medium speed for 2 to 3 minutes, stopping when necessary to scrape down the sides with a spatula; transfer to a medium-sized bowl. Place all the blintz ingredients in the blender and mix well at medium speed for 2 minutes, stopping and scraping down the sides with a spatula when necessary.

In a heavy frying pan or crêpe pan, melt the butter over medium heat; ladle enough batter into the pan to make a medium-sized crêpe. Fry until brown on one side; remove from pan and place on a warm plate. Continue this process, adding butter as needed, and stacking the blintzes as they are made. Drop 2 to 3 tablespoons of the tofu filling onto the fried side of each blintz; turn up the ends toward the center and fold over the sides to enclose the filling. Add another tablespoon of butter to the pan; add the blintzes and fry over medium heat until brown and crispy. Serve immediately with sour cream and honey-sweetened strawberry jam.

Tofu Open Apple Tart

Serves 8

Pastry:
1 cup whole wheat pastry or unbleached white
  flour
1 cup wheat germ
2 heaping tablespoons honey-sweetened
  apricot preserves
¼ teaspoon sea salt
⅓ cup cold-pressed corn oil

Filling:

¼ cup butter

6 large pippin apples, unpeeled and sliced

1½ cups honey-sweetened apricot preserves

½ cup honey

1 pound regular tofu, drained for 20 minutes
   and patted dry

1 teaspoon vanilla

1 teaspoon cinnamon

1 tablespoon sesame tahini (found in Middle
   Eastern or natural food stores)

¼ teaspoon sea salt

Pastry: In a medium-sized bowl, combine all the ingredients and mix until thoroughly blended; press by hand into a 9½-inch pie plate to form a crust. Refrigerate.

Filling: Preheat oven to 350° F. In a large frying pan, melt the butter and remove from heat. Add the apple slices and ½ cup of the apricot preserves, mixing well. Place the pan over medium-low heat, cover, and simmer for 10 minutes or until apples are soft but not mushy. With a slotted spoon, remove the apples and place in a large mixing bowl. Reserve the juice in the frying pan.

In a blender, combine the tofu, honey, vanilla, cinnamon, tahini, salt, and ¼ cup of the apricot preserves; blend at medium speed until smooth and creamy, adding reserved juices as needed to make blending easier. Return the apples to frying pan; add the tofu mixture and stir well.

Remove the crust from the refrigerator and spread with the remaining ¾ cup apricot preserves. Pour in the tofu-apple mixture. Bake for 1 hour. Cool on a wire rack. Refrigerate for at least 4 hours before serving.

VARIATION: Before baking, sprinkle the top of the tofu-apple filling with chopped walnuts and unsweetened, shredded coconut.

Pumpkin Delight

Serves 8

1 16-ounce can pumpkin (if fresh, double the
  amount of spices)
2 pounds regular tofu, drained for 20 minutes
  and patted dry
2 teaspoons vanilla
1 cup honey
¼ teaspoon sea salt
1 teaspoon allspice
1 teaspoon nutmeg
2 teaspoons cinnamon
1 teaspoon pumpkin pie spice
6 rounded tablespoons agar flakes
½ cup hot water
1½ pints whipping cream

Preheat oven to 350° F. Combine the first nine ingredients in a large mixing bowl. Transfer half of the mixture to a blender and mix at medium speed for 2 to 3 minutes until well blended, stopping when necessary to scrape down sides with a spatula. Transfer to a large bowl and mix other half in the blender. Combine all of the blended mixture.

In a small bowl, dissolve the agar in hot water and stir until thickened; stir in 1 cup of the pumpkin-tofu mixture. Add agar to the rest of the mixture. Fold in ½ pint of the whipping cream and mix thoroughly. Carefully pour the mixture into a buttered 9-inch springform pan. Bake for 1 hour. Cool; refrigerate overnight. Gently remove from pan just before serving. Whip the remaining 1 pint of cream for topping.

Tofu Noodle Kugel

A kugel is like a pudding. It can be spiced sweet for a dessert, as this dish is, or made as a main dish simply by changing the seasoning.

    Serves 6 to 8
    1 pound regular tofu, squeezed and crumbled
    3 tablespoons honey
    2 teaspoons cinnamon
    ¼ teaspoon sea salt
    ¼ cup butter, melted
    1 cup golden raisins
    1 cup Thompson raisins
    ½ cup chopped walnuts (optional)
    5 cups cooked noodles, spirals or elbows
        (either corn-soy or whole wheat)

Preheat oven to 350° F. In a medium-sized bowl, combine the tofu, honey, cinnamon, salt and melted butter; mix until thoroughly blended. Add the raisins and nuts, stirring well. Gently add the noodles to the tofu mixture, blending thoroughly with the hands. Pour the mixture into a large buttered casserole or baking dish; bake for 1 hour. Serve hot with whipped cream or ice cream if desired. This kugel is also good cold.

Sweet Potato Pie

Serves 8

Pastry:

1¼ cups whole wheat pastry or unbleached
white flour
½ cup granola
⅛ teaspoon sea salt
⅔ cup non-fat dry milk
½ cup butter
1 teaspoon vanilla
1 egg
⅓ cup honey
2 cups packed shredded coconut
2 teaspoons cinnamon

Filling:

2 sweet potatoes, peeled and cut into ¼-inch-
thick slices
1 pound regular tofu, drained for 20 minutes
and patted dry
1 tablespoon butter
½ cup raisins
½ cup honey
1 teaspoon allspice
1 teaspoon cinnamon

Pastry: In a medium-sized bowl, combine all the pastry ingredients; mix with a pastry blender or the hands. Press two-thirds of the mixture into the bottom and sides of a 9½-inch pie plate, reserving one-third for the top crust.

Filling: Place the sweet potato slices in a steamer or a medium-sized saucepan with 3 to 4 tablespoons water and steam over medium heat for 15 to 20 minutes, or until tender. In a blender, combine the tofu, butter, raisins, honey, allspice and cinnamon; mix at medium speed for 2 to 3 minutes until thoroughly blended, stopping when necessary to scrape down the sides with a spatula.

Preheat oven to 350° F. Layer two-thirds of the steamed sweet potatoes on top of the unbaked pie crust; spread the tofu mixture over the
slices and cover with the remaining one-third of the slices. Press down
remaining pastry on top of the pie, completely covering the filling. Bake
for 25 to 30 minutes. Cool on a wire rack for at least 3 hours before
serving.

Sweet "Cheese" Fritters

These little fritters are simple and very tasty. Accompanied by the apricot
sauce they can serve as a light dessert to end a special meal. Traditionally
the fritters are rolled in powdered sugar after they are fried and drained,
but I found them just as delicious without.

Serves 4 to 6
8 ounces regular tofu, squeezed and crumbled
1 egg
3 tablespoons unbleached white flour
2 tablespoons honey
1 tablespoon orange liqueur
½ teaspoon fresh orange rind, finely grated
Cold-pressed soy or corn oil for deep-frying

Apricot Sauce:
1½ cups honey-sweetened apricot jam
½ cup water
2 tablespoons orange liqueur

In a medium-sized bowl, combine the first six ingredients and beat until
creamy. Refrigerate for at least 4 hours.

When finished refrigerating tofu, prepare the apricot sauce by combin-
ing the jam and water in a small heavy saucepan. Bring to a boil, reduce
heat, and simmer for 5 minutes, stirring constantly. Press the jam through
a sieve; add the liqueur and reheat slowly over low heat.

In a wok or heavy kettle, heat the oil to 375° F. on a deep-fry or candy
thermometer. Shape the tofu batter into walnut-sized mounds with a
spoon and drop into the hot oil; fry until golden brown. Remove and
drain on paper towels or newspaper. Serve immediately with apricot
sauce.

Tofu-Orange Pudding

Serves 4
1 pound regular tofu, drained for 30 minutes,
    patted dry and cut into ½-inch cubes
2 fresh oranges, peeled, seeded, membrane
    removed, and diced
½ to ¾ cup honey
¾ to 1 cup orange juice
1½ teaspoons orange peel, freshly grated
⅛ teaspoon almond extract
Raw slivered almonds to garnish

Place the tofu and oranges in a medium-sized serving bowl and set aside.
    In a saucepan, combine the honey and orange juice and cook, uncovered, over medium heat until reduced to 1 cup. Stir in the orange peel and almond extract; pour over the tofu and gently mix in. Cover and chill for 3 to 4 hours. Sprinkle with almonds just before serving.

Tofu-Honey Custard

Serves 6 to 8
3 eggs
¼ cup honey
¼ teaspoon sea salt
1 cup regular tofu, drained
1 cup milk
1 teaspoon vanilla
½ teaspoon cinnamon
Nutmeg to garnish

Preheat oven to 350° F. In a medium-sized bowl, whisk together the eggs, honey and salt. Place the tofu, milk, vanilla and cinnamon in a blender, and mix at medium speed for 2 to 3 minutes, stopping when necessary to scrape down the sides with a spatula. Whisk the tofu into the egg mixture. Pour into a small casserole and garnish with nutmeg. Bake, uncovered, for 1 hour, or until the custard is firm and a knife inserted in the center comes out clean. Serve warm or cold.

VARIATION: Top the custard with sliced bananas before baking; bake as directed.

Roshmalay

A simple, yet elegant dessert.

Serves 6

1½ pounds regular tofu, squeezed
4 cups whipping cream
1 cup slivered almonds
1½ cups raw sugar
½ teaspoon rose essence (found in Middle
    Eastern stores or kitchen specialty shops)
½ teaspoon vanilla
½ teaspoon mace
¼ teaspoon cardamon
1 cup water

In a medium-sized bowl, crumble the tofu and knead for 5 minutes or until doughy; set aside.

In a medium saucepan, combine the whipping cream, almonds, ½ cup of the sugar, rose essence, vanilla, mace and cardamon. Bring to a boil over medium-low heat and cook, uncovered, for 15 minutes, stirring occasionally; remove from heat, cool completely, and refrigerate.

In a small saucepan, combine the remaining cup of sugar and the water; boil over medium heat for 5 minutes. Shape the tofu into 1-inch balls; dip the balls into the hot sugar syrup and place on a plate, not touching each other. Allow to set for 30 minutes. Gently add the balls to the chilled cream sauce and refrigerate until ready to serve.

Recipe Index